MISSION: POSSIBLE

FOR THE
SMALL CHURCH

Mission Possible for the Small Church

Simplifying Leadership, Structure, and Ministry in Small Churches

©2023 Market Square Publishing, LLC

books@marketsquarebooks.com
141 N. Martinwood, Suite 2 Knoxville, Tennessee 37923

ISBN: 978-1-950899-73-9

Printed and Bound in the United States of America
Cover Illustration & Book Design ©2023 Market Square Publishing, LLC

Editor: Sheri Carder Hood
Post-Process Editor: Ken Rochelle
Cover Design: Kevin Slimp

Table of Contents

Introduction

The small church plays a vital role in many communities across the United States. I (Kay) was born into a small church. After my parents moved our family closer to their jobs due to high gasoline prices in the 1970s, I was raised in another small church. I am a fourth-generation United Methodist and the fourth generation raised in small churches. While my family's earlier generations were part of more rural small churches, my experiences growing up were more small-town, small-church experiences. My faith has been formed through the small church.

The majority of churches in America are small churches. In fact, 70 percent of all congregations have memberships of less than a hundred people, and many are getting smaller. The median attendance has declined every year for the last two decades. It's now less than half of what it was twenty years ago.[1] A 2020 Faith Communities Today (FACT) study shows that half of US congregations have sixty-five people or fewer.[2]

Small churches have an amazing capacity to bounce back over

1 https://storylines.substack.com/p/will-the-pandemic-bring-about-the.

2 https://faithcommunitiestoday.org/fact-2020-survey.

and over again.[3] They are resilient. Since they often have less than a full-time pastor, there is a strong laity leadership preference ready to step in and do what it takes. Small churches also have what we refer to as a superpower that large churches can't touch: the ability to be highly relational from the get-go. Small churches that have discovered and know how to leverage this superpower are vital, healthy churches having God-sized impact in their communities.

Too often, small churches concentrate on what they can't do. We offer this resource to lift up what small churches *can* do! For example, smaller churches have greater percentages of participation, giving, and engaged members than larger churches, according to the 2020 FACT study.[4] Unfortunately, many resources for churches and church leaders are created for larger churches. This resource has been created specifically for the small church.

As we move out of the pandemic into the endemic, postmodern world, many appreciate smaller, more intimate gatherings. In fact, one of the most important things Millennials and Gen Z—the generations missing most from churches—are looking for is authentic community, described as "a culture that fosters authentic community is less about programs, and more about an environment where people care for each other, engage beyond a Sunday, take on the responsibility to look after others' needs, and is open to new people."[5] Wow, doesn't that sound just like the relationships most small churches offer?

To engage the relational superpower, the small church must simplify and clarify its approach to almost everything. Who wants to be tied up in complex church bureaucracy or have no idea how anything operates around the church? A little intentionality will go a long way in the smaller church. In smaller congregations, usually nothing is documented because "how things are done" is

---

[3] https://www.christianitytoday.com/karl-vaters/2019/august/7-reasons-small-churches-are-essential.htm.
[4] https://research.lifeway.com/2021/10/20/small-churches-continue-growing-but-in-number-not-size/.
[5] https://get.tithe.ly/blog/why-cool-church-is-no-longer-working-with-millennials-and-gen-z.

communicated orally. No one has intentionally tried to create complex systems or less-than-transparent processes. It has just happened over time. "It's the way it's always been done."

This resource is designed to help the small church simplify leadership approaches, church decision-making structures, and approaches to ministry. At the same time, it also offers tools to help clarify, focus, and guide small churches so each can operate effectively and efficiently. Ultimately, we hope and pray this resource helps the small church become a lean, relationally-focused, disciple-making movement with greater Kingdom impact!

Gather a small group of leaders to read and study this resource together. "Team Questions" are at the end of each chapter to help you process the topics and ideas and determine the faithful steps you feel called to take for your context. So, let's get started and discover together how to simplify and clarify your ministries to reach more people for Christ.

SECTION
1

Simplified Approaches to Leading
the Small Church

CHAPTER ONE
Leading the Small Church

Blake's father-in-law, Jack, grew up in a family-owned grocery store in a small town in the Arkansas Ozarks. The store was actually featured in a 1955 *Collier's* magazine article titled "The Whittling Capital of America."[6] The lead photo for the article shows the Fendley Produce Company (Cash for Produce, Eggs, Wool, & Hides!) storefront with a row of men whittling on the porch and a hound dog in the foreground.

Eight children were in the family, and most of them had jobs in the grocery store. Jack was the store's butcher for years as a high school and college student. Even when he was in medical school in Little Rock, he would drive to the family store on weekends to carve up the meats and chicken for sale. His average time for butchering a chicken was a speedy twelve seconds. As the family butcher, his job was to carve up the meat quickly, make the presentation as attractive as possible, and ensure that the loyal local customers got exactly the cuts they wanted. Relationships mattered.

Compare his family grocery store experience in the 1960s to the contemporary superstore or the mega market with dozens of staff, a corporate office, an HR department, uniforms, and complex computerized supply-chain systems. Fendley Produce didn't have an

---

6   Ben Lucien Burma, "The Whittling Capital of America," Collier's, September 2,1955.

7

HR department; it had Momma! The kids pitched in after school; everyone had at least a dozen "jobs" to keep the family grocery store running. While you can buy an eight-piece chicken in either store, the customer's experience and the organization's systems are completely different.

Upon reflection, Jack knew the family store could never compete on price (although the cost of driving to the larger neighboring town might make up the difference). He also knew they could never compete on selection (space, cash flow, and food spoilage were limiting factors). But Fendley Produce could always provide superior customer service. The small church is no different! Small churches cannot "compete" with the program offerings of larger churches with multiple paid staff, but they can certainly provide opportunities for deep, caring, Christ-filled relationships! It takes a ton of work for the larger church to manage and offer even a sliver of the relational ministry that is a natural gift of the small church.

The Landscape of the Small Church

It was a social event in the eighteenth century when a new barn needed to be built. There was a barn-raising party! The whole community would come together to build the infrastructure of the new barn. Food and drink were provided. The "family" gathering lasted up to two days, and there was a community expectation that this was an unpaid all-hands-on-deck project. It was also understood that when the time came that you needed help, the favor would be returned. The community took care of one another. While not as common today, barn raisings still do occur.

The small church is very similar. The congregants are all family—sometimes literally, and sometimes the relationships feel as close as family. The small church also operates like a family. They take care of one another, and much of what they do is centered around food. There is a fierce loyalty to the local church—much more so than to the denomination's hierarchy (i.e., district, conference).

Since the congregation is all "family," the whole family often makes the decisions. Everyone perceives they are a member of the Leadership Board and has a vote. However, decisions are heavily influenced by the matriarch or patriarch. This matriarch or patriarch—often attained by birth or marriage—could be a descendant of the first families who planted the church and whose name appears on the church sign, or they could be from an influential family who has kept the church afloat financially. Regardless of how the matriarch or patriarch came to be, sometimes their control is so impenetrable that others wait for the nod from the matriarch or patriarch before speaking up or casting their vote. The matriarch or patriarch does not have to be in a formal leadership position to have substantial influence in a small church.

When it comes to ministry, there is pride in the historical and traditional events. Steeped in tradition, these events require absolutely everyone in the congregation to pull them off. They can't fathom not having these events each year. The forty-second annual turkey dinner is a must-do event, and the annual fall Lord's Acre Sale has been going on for decades. While participation may not be what it once was, the traditional events continue.

Conflicts and Clashes

In any size church, there are conflicts and generational clashes. But conflict is not something to fear or avoid. In fact, a church with no conflict is usually a church that is not really doing much (maybe apathy has set in), or no one dares to do anything new or innovative to rock the boat. A church with no conflict might also signal that no one feels comfortable voicing their opinion or that there is no trust the conflict will be handled in a healthy manner.

It is how conflict is managed that really matters! Healthy management of conflict starts when the church leaders model conflict resolution as taught in Matthew 18:15-20. Second, churches do best to embrace conflict rather than run from it or ignore it. The longer conflict is ignored, the more it grows, and the more others resent the conflict not being addressed. Oftentimes, unresolved conflict results in people leaving the church.

In small churches, family systems theory is usually in play. Therefore, it is important to understand the dynamics of such a system. This informal system of leading and making decisions can be toxic for a church if left unchecked. In their book, *Church Conflict: The Hidden Systems Behind Fights,* Charles Cosgrove and Dennis Hatfield state, "Systems tolerate troublemakers not only to avoid open conflict but also because the group perceives that it derives some benefit from the offending persons and perhaps from their 'unacceptable' behavior."[7] The "troublesome" person who always seems disagreeable and shuts down every new idea may actually be considered by the rest of the church to be a valuable leader who safeguards the church from bad decisions or unsustainable expenses.

According to Cosgrove and Hatfield, a new leader who understands family systems theory and has mapped the informal leadership and the role each plays can use the following four strategies to restructure the church to handle conflict in a healthy manner.

1. **Affiliation**: "Affiliation means identifying oneself positively with a subsystem, whether a person or a group."[8] Find a way to build a bridge relationally and through a shared affinity, identity, and purpose.

---

[7] Charles Cosgrove and Dennis Hatfield, *Church Conflict: The Hidden Systems Behind Fights* (Nashville: Abingdon Press, 1994), 96.

[8] Cosgrove and Hatfield, *Church Conflict,* 133.

2. **Unbalancing Tactics:** To encourage a path out of "stuck-ness," make the issue about ministry programs and not about blaming people. "The aim of such a coalition is to unbalance the system so that it can restructure itself in a way that eliminates the warfare between the two subsystems."[9] Lovingly ask questions, explore the founding purposes of programs and ministries, and inquire about the connection of making disciples who transform the world.

3. **Marking Boundaries:** "Conflict situations develop because unfair boundaries (unfair roles) are assigned to individuals: unchecked and unchallenged, they feel inadequate. Therefore, gifts that God has endowed are not effectively used."[10] When we are expected to work or do ministry beyond our comfort zone or capacity, we stress out and push back. The attentive leader can bring some awareness and balance. Marking boundaries and naming inequities challenge these unfair boundaries and roles.

4. **Joining (affirmation and identification):** "Affirmation means expressing appreciation and praise to others for the things we value about them. Identification means discovering and matching similarities between ourselves and others. As a strategy of joining, identification also means adopting the ways of the family."[11] Pay particular attention and praise those ministries and programs that are effective and vital. Shine a bright light on those who are trying to be faithful and do the right thing but have been marginalized or condemned by bullies. Come alongside the "congregational family" and invest in them relationally.

To help churches stuck in unhealthy family systems, Cosgrove and Hatfield suggest leaders reflect on the scripture below. How

---

9   Cosgrove and Hatfield, *Church Conflict*, 137.

10   https://www.ministrymagazine.org/archive/2009/06/family-systems.

11   Cosgrove and Hatfield, *Church Conflict*, 179.

> *"In making the congregation a spiritual family, the Spirit calls it to reform its natural family life in accord with the new humanity in Christ."*
>
> **Cosgrove and Hatfield**

would this scripture in John guide them to reform their natural family life into a spiritual family in accordance with the new humanity in Christ?

*I pray they will be one,
Father, just as you are in me and I am in you.
I pray that they also will be in us,
so that the world will believe that you sent me.
Indeed we are to more closely align ourselves
to the prayer of Christ that we all may be one.*

John 17:21 (CEB)

Above all, we must be reminded that no one person owns the church, and no one person is in charge of the church. The bottom line is that we are all disciples of Jesus Christ called to live out the Great Commandment and the Great Commission. Jesus commanded us, above all else, to love one another. Jesus declared he would build the church, and our job—the disciples—is to create a movement of people to go tell others the Good News and teach them all that Jesus taught us. Therefore, all decisions should be based on living into this agape love for others and the missional focus Jesus' commanded. When a church is guided with this focus, personal preferences, power struggles, generational clashes, and silos no longer have power or influence. Instead, leaders base decisions on the best way to make disciple-making disciples and show the love of Jesus Christ. When we understand that we are accountable to Christ for leading Jesus' church in its mission of making disciples, suddenly, those conflicts over worship times, those generational clashes around music genres, and the arguments about budgets don't feel so personal. Yet, the responsibility for getting them right for the sake of Kingdom impact suddenly feels heavy and real!

Challenges of Leading the Small Church

The larger church longs for the simpler systems of the small church, and the smaller church longs for the staff of the larger church. The steeple bell always looks shinier at the other church. But, the reality is that there are challenges in leading a church of any size. Here are challenges particular to leading small or family-size churches:

- Because everyone is family or the congregation functions like a family, conflict is difficult in a small church. Conflict is taken personally. What happens in the church is taken to the family birthday parties and other gatherings. There is no separation of the two—it's a family feud.

- Many small churches have become family drive-in chapels. Attenders drive into the facility on Sunday to gather together in the sanctuary where great-grandma still attends or where great-great-grandpa and grandma helped start the church. Those attendees have no other connection to the community. They don't live, shop, eat, or socialize in the community. Therefore, reaching new people in the community is very difficult since they have no ties to the community.

- Likewise, the community doesn't feel connected to the church. Often the church has grown invisible to the community. Someone new might find it difficult to break into the small congregation. It might feel like you showed up to someone else's family Thanksgiving dinner where you knew no one and didn't get all the inside jokes. In these circumstances, evangelism is often nearly, if not completely, nonexistent.

- Because evangelism is often not a superpower of small churches, small churches often get smaller. This is exacerbated as congregants of small churches pass away and family sizes of those belonging to the small churches become smaller. Also, the number of people in the U.S. who

13

associate themselves with a church, synagogue, or mosque has declined from 70 percent in 1999 to 47 percent in 2021.

- Due to its size and budget, the pastor is often part-time, such as quarter-time or half-time. The part-time pastor could be bi-vocational or serving other churches simultaneously in a multi-point charge or a cooperative parish. Due to the pastor's more limited role, relationships (including trust) may not be as strong with the pastor, and appointments may be of shorter duration.

- Finally, implementing almost any change in family systems is often difficult. If change does occur, it normally takes a long time to gain approval, and the motivation for change most often will need to come from inside the family, not outside the family (i.e., pastor, community, new attendee). If change is approved, skepticism will likely still linger, and not everyone will be eager to lend a hand or a dollar to this "crazy" new idea.

Strengths of Leading the Small Church

Leading a small, family-size church also has its strengths and advantages, just like every other size church. Let's take a look at some of those strengths.

- In smaller churches with part-time appointments, the laity step up. Since the pastor is not around full-time, laity assume much of the leadership role, resulting in a strong lay leadership base. There is great commitment and participation.

- In small congregations, everyone knows your name. This is a place for all to feel known. A new person will not attend this church and go unnoticed. Children are loved and nurtured by the whole congregation and afforded opportunities to participate in the church in ways that children in larger churches may not because they are stuck in the "youth annex".

- One can count on routines, schedules, and traditions in the small church. No time is wasted on creating and planning new ministries each year. Everyone knows what is expected of them and what needs to be done. This makes budgeting easier and keeps meetings to a minimum. Activities automatically kick into gear as they have done for years.

- Small family-size churches are simple organizations. It doesn't take multiple meetings and layers of committees to make decisions. While we especially support the use of simplified, accountable structure for all size congregations, small churches almost require use of the leadership model, due to sheer numbers, Since family-size churches are relationally driven, often decisions about the church are made at family functions outside the church where most of the same people are in attendance. Another committee meeting is not required. Gatherings serve double duty.

Every size church has its leadership pros and cons. It is important to be aware of each and navigate them the best you can. Just be sure to keep the purpose of the church—disciple-making—in your sights at all times. As Karl Vaters, author of Small Church Essentials, states, "Small churches are not problems to be fixed, but neither are they an excuse for laziness. Small churches should seek to improve their health while celebrating their unique and significant advantages."[12]

---

[12] Karl Vaters, Small Church Essentials: *Field-Tested Principles for Leading a Healthy Congregation of under 250* (Moody Publishers, March 2018).

Team Questions

1. How are family systems playing out in your small church? How is the family system healthy? What might need to be addressed to support a healthier system?

2. Take inventory of which challenges and strengths from the lists above apply to your church. How can your church build on its strengths?

3. What one challenge, if eliminated, could have the most positive impact on the vitality of your church? How might your church work to eliminate the challenge in the upcoming year?

CHAPTER TWO
Pastoring in the Small Church

Upon reflection, a new pastor of a rural family chapel had a difficult first Sunday: "I held a church meeting in the sanctuary immediately after worship to tell everyone that we needed to plan programs for the fall season. I just told everyone to sit down after the benediction, and I led the meeting. They didn't seem all that interested in what I told them we needed to do." Ouch!

This book comes, in part, from conversations such as these with pastors seeking to serve the unique needs and opportunities of small churches. Many books, articles, and online posts about church leadership were designed for larger churches—ones with staff, multiple programs, and one or more full-time clergy. Clergy have been taught that the pastor is the "CEO" of the church and needs to take charge accordingly. That's fine, and when I (Blake) served a larger church, I was appreciative of these approaches, but much of this guidance to pastors simply ignores the reality of the pastor serving the small church. We are told to "hire for our weaknesses"—awesome advice I have followed, staffing a large church to compensate for my manifold weaknesses.

Pastors are told to set aside a full day for sermon writing and a week each year to plan our annual sermon and worship series. Pastors are encouraged to guide church leaders in a strategic planning process to map out and clearly articulate the congregation's mission, vision, and SMART (specific, measurable, achievable, relevant, & time-based) goals, along with building processes and programs to welcome guests, integrate them into the congregation, and disciple them with an intentional system. While this is wonderful advice for a clergy leader of a larger church, none of this advice can be used in the small church—at least not without serious adaptation. Small churches are simply different.

The role of the pastor is expressed distinctively in different-sized congregations. In larger congregations, the lead pastor takes on a stronger vision-casting role, with leadership functions (planning, staff management, board development, and stewardship) taking up a greater percentage of the pastor's time.

In mid-sized churches, the pastor and the board must always negotiate and clarify their respective roles and responsibilities, with "governance" and "management" feeling like points on a spectrum rather than a clear-cut binary. For instance, while the pastor may have the "right" to terminate an employee in the by-laws, the reality is that prior notice to the board and the presence of a member of the board or the personnel committee may be expected for any disciplinary action with an employee. The role of the pastor in a small church is particularly different from that expressed in many church leadership books in that small church pastors who attempt to be the vision-casters, CEOs, or ministry managers will often soon discover that they have overplayed their hands.

Programs and buildings don't make disciples. God uses disciples to make disciples. Small churches, you have a special gift: you can make Jesus Christ personal. In the fall of 2020, amid COVID shutdowns, Blake's daughter went out of state to begin college. If you ask him, he wasn't worried she would have problems finding a church with all sorts of programs and a great rock band. He was worried about how she would discover a soul-nurturing Christian community while wearing a mask everywhere and where all the normal ways to gather and connect thousands of students had been shut off.

Instead of leading through complexity with programs and systems, the pastor of the small church ministers and leads through relationships. Intimacy is a superpower of the small congregation, and fruitful ministry must flow from this incredibly powerful source.

In the story that began this chapter, the new pastor led with programming and power instead of engaging through relationships. It is like trying to use iPhone skills on an Android phone. Sure, the similarities are there, but the operating system is simply different, and you will get a result you didn't expect. This pastor received only blank stares and a stern parking-lot conversation with the chair of the Pastor-Parish Relations Committee. The pastor tried to assume authority that the pastor didn't have to create processes the church didn't comprehend before investing in the relationship-building that is the lifeblood of the congregation.

Pastoring from the Porch Swing – The Family Chapel

Beginning in the early 1980s, church consultants and sociologists diligently studied the relationship between church size and how the church operated. Categories have been defined and redefined over the past few decades, but much of the work still holds validity because, at their root, the categories were less about culture, methods, or technologies and more about human nature. People simply engage each other differently in different-sized institutions.

One of the learnings that has held up considerably well is that a small church usually has an unofficial matriarch or patriarch who embodies the organizing principles of the church. They may or may not hold elective office in the church anymore, but they carry a deep sense of the congregation's identity, the giftedness of the people,

19

and the calling of the church. In recent years, with the changing of the generations, we have seen several churches that have lost their matriarch or patriarch due to death or disability. Sometimes the unofficial matriarch or patriarch position is seamlessly passed on to another member who is respected enough to inherit the responsibility. But we have also seen the mantle lay unclaimed, which can be quite anxiety-producing in a small congregation.

We begin this section about "pastoring the family chapel" by discussing the role of laity because the pastor's role in this small church of under forty engaged congregants truly begins with the identity and culture of the laity, not the actions or initiative of the pastor. Instead of building programs, structuring processes for ministry, or casting a vision and articulating the church's mission, the pastor of the family chapel is a coach. Blake wrote about this approach in a 2021 article for *Ministry Matters*:[13]

> *The smaller the church, the more the pastor's leadership exists outside the committee meeting room or even behind the pulpit. Instead the leader rests on the metaphorical porch swing. In my home state, Arkansas, especially in the evening, we enjoy banter from the front porch swing. You sit side-by-side on a porch swing. You can't sit in the adversarial position across from someone, hoping to win them over or tire them out. Side-by-side it is, looking in the same direction, leaning over and talking with each other, loving each other as fellow servants of God.*
>
> *Porch swings foster curiosity: What is that we are seeing in front of us? "Tell me what the town was like when you were growing up . . . What was the church like then?" Rather than managers, small churches need spiritual leaders and nurturers who love the congregation and the community where it is planted. Instead of setting a leadership agenda, porch-swing leadership . . . looks a lot more like coaching a participatory sports team.*

---

[13] Blake Bradford, "Leading the Small Church from the Porch Swing," *Ministry Matters,* October 17, 2021, https://www.ministrymatters.com/lead/entry/11074/leading-the-small-church-from-the-porch-swing.

*While it may seem like it takes more time, porch-swing
leadership is also empowering, because leading from the porch
swing allows pastors to process ideas, opportunities, and
challenges alongside the lay leadership, working out the critical
elements of context, history, capacity, and "fit-ness" before any
formal decision is even considered, much less voted upon. While
things may need to simmer for a while as you rock on the porch
together, in the end, the lay leader may lean over and say, "Pastor,
that just might work. Let's go for it!"*

One of our hopes for this book is that it will be read by small-
church laity and clergy together as you rock on the porch swing
alongside one another, lifting up possibilities and opportunities that
will fit into your context.

One pastor, originally from Texas, uses a bit of a different
metaphor. Once a pastor who worked with rural small-church
cooperative parishes but now works in a suburban small-church
cooperative parish, he refers to this approach as (cue the Southern
accent) "drinking sweet tea." He suggests the pastor drink a lot of
sweet tea with their congregants to build relationships, gain trust,
learn the history of the church and the community, and hear their
hopes and dreams. Of course, we know it doesn't really matter the
beverage or seating choice; it is all about investing in a mutual
relationship.

In these metaphors, notice that the work of pastoral care,
leadership, and discipleship are intermingled. Deep issues of faith,
congregational priorities, community needs, and family concerns
are interwoven into a tapestry of meaningful conversation,
mirroring the rich complexity of meaning, frailty, and giftedness
that every one of us carries in our soul. If intimacy is a superpower
of the small congregation, porch-swing leadership plugs directly into
this giftedness.

Of course, one can't sit and rock on the porch swing forever. Jesus did tell us to "Therefore go . . ." in the Great Commission! That leads us to the second half of pastoral leadership in the family chapel: simply showing up and offering a ministry of presence. Blake uses the metaphor of being a co-laborer in God's field from 1 Corinthians 3 in his *Ministry Matters* article from 2021:[14]

> *Some leadership happens in the garden of service, including the nurture of discipleship formation, outreach, and caregiving for our neighbors. In the small-town or rural church, leave behind the role expectations of the program director, which in some churches can feel like a "cruise-ship activities director."*
>
> *Instead, the pastoral leader is a co-laborer in God's garden. In the garden of discipleship service, working side-by-side, clergy and laity plant ministry seeds. Pastors guide the congregation as it does some necessary weeding and pruning of existing ministries that either require too many resources or have not shown fruit. While painful at the moment, pruning ministries will be an indispensable tool as we recover from COVID and all the challenges it has added to our church and community life. And as ministries bring forth fruit, it is pastors who can encourage the congregation as we share stories of success, fruitfulness, and God's mighty works in our neighborhoods and towns.*

In his article, Blake links together a ministry of presence and the leadership needs of the congregation to prune ministries. This is a careful dance. By working together, the lay leaders and pastor must carefully consider how ministries need to adapt to our current era. In our work with hundreds of congregations, we have found no congregation that can continue to do business as usual as if it were still 2019. Every church needs to reassess, prune ministries, and adapt to the reality we now find ourselves in.

---

14 Bradford, "Leading the Small Church from the Porch Swing."

Frankly, this ongoing accountability assessment should have existed long before in congregations and been a practice as ingrained as breathing amongst leaders. But the work of pruning is required now for any chance at sustainability, much less fruitfulness. Pastors, keep asking questions. Laity, drop your defensiveness. This is not about blame or what used to work. The world has changed; we can't expect our beloved ministries to ignore reality.

I (Kay) suggest that every ministry has an expiration date. Many churches keep their ministries on hospice and life support because they just can't let them go. It's time to lovingly let them go. Celebrate the ministry, the ones who birthed and nurtured it, and the fruitfulness it once brought. Give it a beautiful funeral, and then let it rest in peace. The pastor can use her role as "officiant" to help a congregation say goodbye.

For example, I (Blake) consulted with a church known in the community for its annual pumpkin patch. But their attendance had dwindled. The personnel required to host a multi-week pumpkin patch was unsustainable. Finally, a bad pumpkin crop forced them to rethink their annual event and convert it into an incredibly successful afternoon fall festival organized in cooperation with the public elementary school a few blocks away.

Looking back on the endeavor, the leaders told me how frustrated they were at themselves that it took an "agricultural intervention" to do the accountability work they should have performed years earlier. They had lost sight of the purpose of the pumpkin patch (to connect with the neighborhood). The strain of the logistics, planning, and implementation had exhausted their congregation. Now, by some pruning and a little "repotting" of the ministry, they rediscovered the joy of community connections and reconnected with the local school. Where is the pastor in all of this? Asking the right questions. Encouraging the leaders as they make the hard call. Serving at the festival by meeting folks. Celebrating the ministry's fruitfulness and the laity's leadership.

Pastoring from the Switchboard – The "Big" Small Church

In congregations with fifty to seventy-five active congregants, the role of the pastor is more complex than the coach and preacher needed by the smaller family chapel. In the "larger" small churches, the emotional and organizing role of the matriarch/patriarch may be realized through multiple members. Along with that change, the pastor begins to serve as a switchboard function, linking together groups, families, committees, and ministries. In church consultant workshops, with slides projected on the wall of the fellowship hall, you will often see a chart with the pastor pictured in the center like a hub with all these groups and individuals linking through the pastor. Blake uses historical images from the 1950s telephone switchboards and modern computer routers in these workshops to symbolically describe the pastor's role. Other times, he refers to the pastor of this size church as the "circuit breaker."

One reason these metaphors prove difficult to comprehend is that the very nature of the pastor's role in this size church is incredibly challenging. Switchboard operators get overwhelmed, circuit breakers burn out and meltdown. In the church, when everything— including conflict—runs through the pastoral circuit breaker, the system gets overloaded. Sadly, there have been more than enough meltdowns and overloaded circuits. Many pastors have shared with us that, while they may not be burned out, they sure feel crispy.

The churches in this category often sit uncomfortably at an exciting-yet-somewhat-challenging transition point. They teeter on the line of appropriateness for full-time or part-time clergy while balancing the struggle of resourcing ministry. This balancing act is complicated by the fact that managing all the people and groups can be incredibly taxing for pastors and churches that seek to focus on relational ministry. It is sometimes a difficult tipping point to move past. Fear can retract the church's growth and vitality. But branching out with faith and vision can often cause a breakthrough that moves the church past the tipping point. So, first, we encourage all involved to have grace for one another.

The pastor, church, and judicatory staff should collaborate on the sustainable vision for the church. The financial difference in compensation costs between full-time and part-time clergy is enormous. Congregations at this uncomfortable "middle place" will need to figure out how to place funding for the pastor (and all the expectations attached) alongside other priorities such as ministry, facilities, and fixed costs. A host of contextual factors will be a part of this decision, and both choices can be faithful missional options. Please note, however, that the church will need to seriously adjust its expectations if it chooses to shift from a full-time to a less-than-full-time pastor. The relational "switchboard" functions must be shared amongst lay leadership working collaboratively while the pastor's role becomes more intentionally defined.

What can only the (Part-time) Pastor Do?
Setting Realistic Clergy Expectations for the Bi-vocational, Retired, or Shared Pastor

As a judicatory executive responsible for assigning pastors to churches, I (Blake) have often found myself negotiating realistic expectations for a pastor serving a less-than-full-time appointment. For the new clergy who are often bi-vocational, I make it clear that they are always clergy, even if they are not "on duty." Certain expectations—particularly moral expectations and an expectation for being reasonably available in pastoral emergencies—are never time-bound, even if the pastor is not on the clock in their quarter-time or half-time appointment. But the church with a pastor serving less than full time must organize its priorities and goals for the pastor's time accordingly.

For congregations who have experienced only a full-time pastor, adjusting expectations for their first part-time clergyperson feels monumental. While I, as their district superintendent, make it clear that their pastor is "always their pastor," I also must help these congregations adjust to their new reality. We know it's hard. Adapting from having a full-time pastor who is always present, available, and living in-residence in their local parsonage to being led by a bi-vocational, retired, or shared pastor, especially one that lives outside the community, can bring an emotional impact along with huge practical alterations to a congregation's life.

So, what are reasonable expectations for a pastor serving less than full-time? It is best to start with a question, not a to-do list: "What can only your pastor do?" If a pastor only has a handful of hours to do "church work," what is the best use of that time? I suppose we can start with sacramental responsibilities. Then add weekly preaching and worship leadership (along with their requisite preparation and posting on social media). Include some pastoral care and a Bible study. Tuck in an hour for organizing the food pantry or other mission and maybe another hour to visit that nice couple who visited last Sunday. Insert some time for governance and leadership (committee meetings), and then spend a little time on administration (because large or small, nonprofit institutions always require paperwork). Let's also not forget educational requirements, such as course-of-study programs for United Methodist licensed local pastors. How is that ten hours a week looking? There is an old seminary maxim that a preacher should spend an hour writing for every minute of preaching. At this rate, the congregation might get a forty-five-second sermon to match the forty-five minutes available for the pastor to actually write the sermon!

So, let's get realistic. "What can only your pastor do?" In the Methodist tradition, the answer is to preside over the sacraments and serve as the administrative officer. Even these two responsibilities can be creatively imagined. For instance, if the church understands that congregational caregiving is the role of the entire congregation (a part of living out our discipleship), then the pastor's role, as part of a larger team approach, can be focused on uniquely pastoral responsibilities such as bringing communion to individuals and families. As for being the administrative officer, such a role does not require the pastor to actually do the church's administrative work but to be an accountability partner to ensure the individuals responsible for the work completes their duties.

A similar lens can be used on every aspect of the congregation's life when assessing the *real* expectations for the small-church pastor. It does take some reorganization of thinking. Small congregations often speak of paying for the preacher every Sunday. This reference attaches compensation to only the Sunday sermon instead of the overall servant ministry of the clergyperson. That's not helpful; a pastor is a radically different job than a supply preacher. We need to decouple compensation from the weekly sermon when referring to the pastor's work, especially in the small congregation.

Preachers are well aware that every year has fifty-two Sundays. Focusing so much of the part-time pastor's limited availability on the Sunday sermon may actually be holding your church back from the greater gifts a pastor can bring to a church. Look at the fifty-two Sundays from a wider lens. While the pastor may preach the vast majority of these Sundays, can arrangements be made for other uses of the pastor's time over the year if some sermon time during worship is used in alternative ways? A congregation can reimagine the sermon time to include several Sundays every year for alternatives to the pastor-led sermon: member testimonies, musical services or hymn sings, youth/children Sundays, service Sundays in the community, and focused prayer times. These are not about extra "clergy vacation days" but are about using the pastor's service time differently. Also, there is another benefit: the congregation itself is strengthened by using its spiritual gifts more fully!

Expectation-setting needs to be regrounded in a realistic assessment of the pastoral role in ministries and church life. If the last pastor was the only one willing to show up to organize the food pantry, fill the blessing box, teach the Bible study, or run the community youth group, then some serious conversation needs to occur before assigning these tasks to the new pastor. Perhaps these were not your church's ministries but the personal ministry passions of the disciple of Jesus that happens to serve as your pastor. If the church isn't excited about these ministries, it's okay to pause them, regroup, and figure out what the signature ministry of the congregation is so the whole congregation can get involved in that ministry.

As the leadership considers the signature ministry, acknowledge that the pastor doesn't need to be present every time the ministry happens. Similarly, committee meetings, men's and women's group gatherings, and other meetings should be considered optional for the part-time pastor. On a seasonal basis, the leadership should work with the pastor to identify and designate which meetings, gatherings, and activities require a pastoral presence to build relationships, community presence, or a better congregational understanding and help the pastor focus on those gatherings. It also helps to simplify the church's life. You have already read about the need for a simplified, accountable structure. As you consider the time expectations for the pastor, consider the huge difference between asking the pastor to attend a single monthly Leadership Board meeting as opposed to the time sunk into multiple sequential committee meetings.

Team Questions

1. In collaboration with the pastor, make a list of all the tasks the pastor performs in the average month.

2. Next to each task, estimate the time involved in completing it every month and compare it to the schedule and available time of the part-time or full-time pastor. How does it compare?

3. Looking at the original list of tasks, prioritize what is most important, what can be laid aside, and what is best performed by a disciple?

4. What is one learning from this exercise that might help the pastor and congregation serve Christ more fruitfully together?

CHAPTER THREE

Accountable Leadership: Thumping the Melon

Arkansas is proud of its watermelons. When I (Blake) began full-time ministry, I was appointed to the border city of Texarkana, near the little town of Hope, home of the annual Watermelon Festival (since 1926!). When picking your watermelon, you need to check if it's ripe. So you pick it up, cradle it in your arms like a beloved watermelon baby, and then thump it with your knuckles. It is ready to eat if it gives a nice hollow, deep tone that you feel throughout the melon.

Step into any produce section of a grocery store, and you will see folks testing the fruit. Is it ripe? Is it spoiled? Are the bumps simply surface imperfections, or are they bruises that have deeply impacted the fruit? Every fruit has slightly different criteria, and consciously or unconsciously, we test the fruit, holding it into account. Of course, accountability is not limited to fruit and is an integral part of discipleship and church leadership.

I (Kay) often offer my sense of ultimate accountability as a church leader in workshops by thinking about it in these terms: imagine getting to the pearly gates (hoping and still working to get there) and being asked the question, "How did you lead the church on your watch?" That's the ultimate question for accountable church leadership. Ultimately, as members of the Leadership Board, we are given authority (by the congregation through the election at charge conference) and have taken responsibility to ensure the church is living its purpose, as Jesus proclaimed in the Great Commission to go and make disciples and train them in Jesus' ways so that the world will be transformed.

Accountable Leadership as an Act of Stewardship

In a church culture where we often do ministries "just because..." (i.e., *just because* it sounds charitable, or *just because* Mrs. Matriarch wants to, or *just because* we always have done it that way), accountable leadership feels radical. Rarely do we create ministries with the transformational impact in mind and work backward from that goal. For some reason, there is a belief that because the church is made up mostly of "volunteers," no one can be held accountable. (As an aside, we never use the term *volunteers* and instead prefer the term *serving disciples*). Think about that for a minute. If this life is preparing us for eternal life, where did we ever come up with the idea that accountability for fruitfulness in the life of the church and as a disciple is not reasonable? Should this not be the place where we are held most accountable?

We are Wesleyans, and Methodist Christians have accountability hardwired into us from our history of class meetings, early societies, and conferences. The early Methodist societies always kept count of members, money, and ministry. While we may think of annual conference as a business meeting, revival, or equipping event, its origins were as an annual accountability tool: How many new class meetings and bands (small groups) were formed? How many souls were reached for Christ? How well were our traveling preachers leading the expansion of the church into new territory for new people? We can recover that meaningful accountability today. That is, if we are willing to start with our end in mind (impactful transformation) and then work backward from our goal while maintaining a culture of accountability under the stewardship of the new Leadership Board.

Over the years, when a church is considering simplifying its governance structure but is unable or unwilling to begin practicing accountability, we have recommended that the church *not* move into simplification—with the exception of churches in hospice mode wrapping up their temporal business. That being said, we realize that small-membership churches are often moving into simplification by the sheer fact of math meeting demographics. This should not relieve the church from practicing accountable leadership, however.

Accountability marries *responsibility* and *authority*. In other words, accountable leadership is when a person is given the responsibility and authority for a job, project, or ministry, and then the board, pastor, or team leader holds the person accountable for the intended and agreed-upon outcome. We know that small-membership congregations, whose lifeblood is relationships, are wary of accountability in church work because leaders worry that accountability will strain relationships.

Accountability often gets a bum rap because it is often confused with blaming or disciplinary actions. Yet, blaming is quite different from accountability. While accountability connects responsibility and authority, blaming usually occurs when someone has responsibility but no actual authority or capacity to fulfill the expectations. Accountability isn't about disciplinary action or punishment. Rather, accountability is about support, encouragement, and learning. Practicing accountability means identifying needed resources, uncovering roadblocks, and clarifying how to get back on track.

When I (Blake) was a congregational coach, I often asked the pastor and lay leaders about the relationship between authority and responsibility in the congregation. Sadly, I observed too many situations in which the two were tenuously connected, if at all. I also remember asking a leader who was responsible for a particular ministry, and he said, "Well, we all sort of team up for that. It's less about titles and job descriptions; we just get it done. So I guess everyone is responsible." While I understand and sympathize with the sentiment, holding "everyone accountable" for a project is hard, if not impossible. If everyone is responsible, no one is responsible.

In larger churches, accountability needs to be organized into a system. In small-membership churches, it needs to be enculturated with some simple values. Think of accountability as stewardship: how are we making sure that every donated dollar and every disciple's hour invested in the church's mission is being invested and used well to build up God's kingdom?

Who Holds Who Accountable?

Every disciple is accountable to Jesus Christ, and corporately, as the body of Christ called the church, we are all accountable to Christ's mission. The first entity that a Leadership Board must hold accountable is itself. As the governing board, it has both the responsibility and authority to lead. The governing board is accountable to God to fulfill Christ's mission and to use its authority to hold the pastor and the rest of the church accountable to Christ's mission as well.

The Leadership Board is accountable to Christ (the owner of the church) for the church being faithful in fulfilling its mission of making disciples of Jesus Christ for the transformation of the world (the Great Commission). Accountability is not a "one-and-done" evaluation. It needs to be the culture. We've created a simple chart to outline the cycle of accountable leadership.

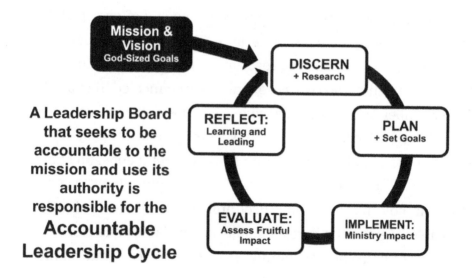

A Leadership Board that seeks to be accountable to the mission and use its authority is responsible for the **Accountable Leadership Cycle**

Mission & Vision — God-Sized Goals

DISCERN + Research

PLAN + Set Goals

IMPLEMENT: Ministry Impact

EVALUATE: Assess Fruitful Impact

REFLECT: Learning and Leading

Accountable Leadership Cycle	
Mission, Vision, & Purpose (God-sized Goals)	Ministries should come out of the church's mission, vision, and goals. Accountability is ultimately rooted in following Christ's mission for the congregation.
Discern + Research	The first step of the cycle is to discern ministry needs as rooted in the mission. Discernment takes prayerful conversation and research such as demographic studies, neighborhood prayer walks, conversations with local community leaders such as the school principal or mayor, and listening to neighbors.
Plan + Set Ministry Goals	The ministry team and coordinator should plan and set goals for the proposed ministry, including the purpose of the ministry, intended outcome, and trackable measurements. For example, a "bridge event" to connect to unchurched neighbors (purpose) and to meet our neighbors so we can build new relationships (intended outcome) by having an attendance of 75 people, collecting names and contact information for 30 people, and following up with three touch points in the next 30 days (trackable measurements). To successfully implement this relational event, we will need plans for congregants to greet and get to know guests, not just "run the event." In addition, people willing, equipped, and ready to engage in follow-up and relationship-building with the neighbors must be ready to go. Don't wait until after the event to recruit and equip these people. They also need to outline exactly what those three touches will be and have those resources (i.e., notecards and stamps or flyers) or next steps (invitations for one-on-one coffee) identified and ready to go. Ministries without planned goals for transformational impact become random "feel-good events." The ministry team should create clear goals with intended outcomes as part of its ministry planning.
Implement: Ministry Impact	The responsible ministry team is now ready to execute the plan using the predefined goals. Ultimately, every serving disciple on the team (and the church) is accountable to the mission of the particular ministry and the congregation's larger overall mission and vision. Impactful ministries seek to make disciple-making disciples who transform the world.

Evaluate: Assess Fruitful Impact	The ministry team should assess the ministry from proposal to event to follow-up to thank-you notes. What worked well? What needed work? What surprised the team? What was the Kingdom impact? Using the goals for the ministry, how did the ministry measure up? What did the team learn? Were there any Holy Spirit sightings during the ministry? This evaluation is a vital step in accountability. Don't put off the evaluation! Gather the team within a week of the event to evaluate. If there are still parts of the implementation in play (i.e., follow-up over the next thirty days in our bridge event example), evaluate the event immediately. Then re-gather at the end of the 30-day follow-up period to evaluate that portion of the ministry. If the ministry is ongoing, evaluate it at least twice a year.
Reflect: Learning and Leading	A solid evaluation allows the coordinator and pastor to learn about the mission field and the congregation's capacity for ministry follow-through. This reflection time is different from an evaluation. While an evaluation is about doing things right, reflection is about doing the right things. This may even be a time of reflection for both individual ministry reflection and reflection on ministries collectively. How are the ministries related and helping create energy or momentum for one another? Or are they completely disconnected and trying to reach entirely different demographics? Would our resources have more impact if our ministries were more related or if we were to realign our ministries for the same targeted demographic? Reflection is a skill and an intentional practice that invites the congregation's leaders back into the season of prayerful learning and discernment about the congregation's future.

Adapted from Kay Kotan and Blake Bradford's *Mission Possible 3+*, page 124, and Blake Bradford's *Strengthening Decision-Making and Governance*, page 72.

The Accountable Leadership Cycle can be used throughout the church to maintain alignment and accountability. For instance, a pastor can use it when meeting with whoever is coordinating a ministry. The VBS organizer can use it with the team helping to host Vacation Bible School. Regardless of church size, we disciples are not being called just to keep our church doors open or to be event planners.

We are called to make disciples of Jesus and make transformational Kingdom impact in individual lives and in our communities and neighborhoods. Every watermelon needs to be thumped!

Setting goals (expected outcomes and results) for ministries might feel too corporate for your church, but goals don't have to be complicated. A goal of the VBS might be to connect meaningfully with one family that doesn't have a church home. Goals create a compelling purpose that will attract more congregational energy and remind everyone of the purpose of a specific ministry. For instance, if we know that a goal of a fall festival is to get the names of guests and do excellent follow-up, we will organize the ministry very differently than if we didn't include that evangelistic element. What might have been just a nice event for the neighborhood becomes a disciple-making bridge event to build relationships. Having a clear understanding of the expected outcome matters!

When I (Blake) was a scout in the mid-1980s, a popular trip for the troop was going to Philmont Scout Ranch in New Mexico for a multiday backpacking adventure. One of the first tasks when arriving, and well before starting the hike, was to unload all the backpacks and lay out every single item on the ground. This practice is called a "shakedown." In backpacking, ounces matter, and a solid shakedown means only essential gear is taken on the journey. A few extra ounces add up to a few extra pounds of gear, which could mean a lot of pain and difficulty on the trail. Shakedowns were not designed to embarrass anyone, and no scout was supposed to get bent out of shape when some items were removed from their bag. Everyone knew that a proper shakedown was needed to benefit the whole troop.

Churches of all sizes are great at stuffing backpacks full of ministries, events, and layered expectations. We scarcely have a new event without the title "First Annual" being attached. Over time, these ministries wax and wane in fruitfulness and participation. The mission field needs change. Leaders arrive with different callings and ministry passions. We start maintaining ministries more out of nostalgia and fear than mission and fruitfulness. Small-membership congregations are not immune to this.

I recall visiting with leaders of a small church where almost every active adult member had a key to a different closet in the church. Members were each doing a "private" ministry that they were excited about and had their own closet for supplies. These dozen leaders were loath to work together on any ministry project, preferring instead to "do their own thing." Of course, this all proved unsustainable! Small churches need one or two signature ministries in which everyone, young and old, can be involved together in ministry. Part of accountability is knowing that some ministries need to be concluded or unplugged from life support. The small-church pastor rarely has the authority to end a ministry, so the Leadership Board needs to step up.

Our congregations need a ministry shakedown. When Blake served as a congregational coach and equipper for his judicatory office, one of his gut-check tools (to see how serious a church's leadership was about missional fruitfulness) was to ask about the last few ministries that were shut down for ineffectiveness. The question often prompted quizzical looks. People seem to think that *ministries* are granted eternal life, not disciples. But if we are really holding ministries accountable to our mission and vision, then a certain number of these ministries will be ineffective and require a relaunch, rethink, or memorial service. "Well done, good and faithful ministry! You made an impact for Christ, and your season is now over." A proper ministry shakedown means there is more space left over in your church's backpack for new ministries that are relevant and impactful.

Evaluating ministries as an ongoing practice and regular ministry shakedowns ensures your congregation is ready and resourced to make disciples and transform your community and the world. Don't get stuck maintaining yesterday's ministries at the expense of God's calling today, let alone God's preferred future for your church.

TEAM QUESTIONS

1. How does your current board or Church Council hold ministries accountable to the mission and vision of the church?

2. When was the last time your church intentionally shut down (or put on evaluative "pause") a ministry for being ineffective or no longer missionally aligned? Reflect on how it was done and how you might do it differently now.

3. What is one change you can make now to encourage a culture of accountability in discipleship and leadership?

CHAPTER FOUR
Contextual Leadership

Every small church is unique, especially given their context. In this chapter, we will describe some of the nuances of the small church in rural areas, towns, and cities.

A small church in a city or town is very different from a small church in a rural area. In rural areas, people are used to driving distances to do almost anything. I (Kay) have worked with rural churches whose members travel nearly an hour to purchase groceries, and the nearest gas station is twenty miles away. The mission field (the geographic area the church has identified, claimed, and takes responsibility for reaching the people who live within the area) for rural churches is typically much larger than in other settings. It could be a zip code, multiple zip codes, a twenty-minute drive, or even an entire county or two.

In contrast, small churches in more densely populated areas are used to having quicker access to modern conveniences and choices. What this small-church demographic is looking for in a faith community is likely quite different from that of an isolated rural setting. Mission field sizes in these settings are usually much smaller than in rural settings and are usually about a ten-minute walk from the church's facility. However, the more densely populated the area is, the smaller the mission field is for the church. There are real indicators and natural transitions from one neighborhood to the next. One can usually "feel" when a person moves from one neighborhood to another. These natural boundaries help determine mission-field parameters.

Most churches identify way too large of a mission field. There is a false assumption that the larger the mission field and the resulting associated population identified, the easier the reach will be for new people. The truth is that the smaller the mission field is, the easier it is for the church to understand and identify their closest neighbors, and in turn, this should make reaching the neighbors easier. When the church chooses too large of a mission field (geographically and/or population), identifying more specifically who the neighbor is across the street or around the corner is lost in the vastness of the thousands of other people and information the report is showing. As a general rule of thumb, shoot for a mission field with a population of approximately ten-thousand people as a starting point.

The Rural Small Church

One of the inherited maxims is that there is a United Methodist Church in almost every county and zip code in America. Vital rural churches anchor communities, joining schools, libraries, and hospitals, the eponymous company behind the company towns. In sociology, *anchor institutions* are the enduring, geographically fixed, mission-focused, and trusted nonprofit, governmental, or even for-profit entities that provide the backbone of a community's health and identity.

Rural churches are remarkable anchor institutions. Many have existed for over a century, often in the same location, with a rootedness that makes them an inseparable part of the fabric of a community's life. We need to back up a little bit, though. What is a rural church? Ann Michel of the Lewis Center for Church Leadership at Wesley Theological Seminary interviewed Allen Stanton, the

Turner Center executive director at Martin Methodist College. Stanton is an ordained United Methodist Church minister and the author of *Reclaiming Rural: Building Thriving Rural Congregations*.[15] In this 2021 interview for the Leading Ideas newsletter, Rev. Stanton shared that there is no stereotypical rural church and described how expectations and the usual definitions of vitality need to be adjusted for a rural small-church setting:

> *We can't even agree on what "rural" means. The federal government has 15 different definitions of a rural community. I live in a rural community and attend a county seat church full of lawyers and doctors and bankers. You also have rural churches on back roads with 15 or 30 people. There's no way to say, "This is what a rural church is." You have to look at the nuances of each congregation to figure out what vitality means in that context. . . .Part of this is the way we define vitality. There have been efforts to come up with one standard definition of church vitality. The problem is that these are often weighted towards suburban and urban churches. . . .So, we have to figure out the actual demographics of a particular rural community and not just default to what worked in a suburban place or an urban place. Rural places are not just like little urban communities. They're different. They behave differently.[16]*

The United Methodist Church has historically been able to support and maintain churches in rural America, even in communities where local schools have been consolidated (or disappeared) and their longtime local businesses bought out. An especially challenging factor in American rural life is the closing of local hospitals. All these factors mean a loss of access to services and economic benefits and a drain on professionals and their families.

---

[15] Allen Stanton, *Reclaiming Rural: Building Thriving Rural Congregations*, (Rowman and Littlefield, 2021).
[16] Allen T. Stanton and Ann A. Michel, "Building Thriving Rural Congregations" (September 14, 2021), https://www.churchleadership.com/leading-ideas/building-thriving-rural-congregations/.

Often, the local church is the only remaining anchor institution left standing. Beth Hatcher, then a staff writer for the Institute for Emerging Issues at North Carolina State University, interviewed United Methodist Church pastors Cliff Wall and James Henderson, along with research fellow Kylie Foley, for an article on churches and rural America.

> When it takes 20-30 minutes to get anywhere and your town doesn't even have a stoplight, sometimes the church is all folks have got. That's certainly the case in Harmony, NC, the small Iredell County town, pop. 533, where Clarksbury United Methodist Church is located. The church fills in the gaps of often absent or hard-to-reach social services, whether it's repairing a congregation member's roof, providing free health screenings or planning the summer reading program. . . ."Our life as Christians is a life of relationships, not only to God, but to people," [Pastor] Wall said.
>
> This multifaceted relationship to the community has been crucial throughout the church's history. "Rural congregations have often been in their communities for decades, even hundreds of years. Faith communities were often the first institutions established in a new community," said Kylie Foley, IEI's Rural Faith Communities Fellow. "Faith leaders would ride around rural areas, spreading news and information, connecting separate communities across a variety of differences."
>
> "The African-American church has been a haven for Black folks," said Pastor James Henderson, who pastors three central North Carolina United Methodist churches. Up until the mid-20th century, widespread segregation often silenced African-Americans in mainstream discourse, especially in the rural South. The church gave the community a voice, and a place to speak freely. Instrumental in the Civil Rights Movement, rural African-American faith communities remain key community centers, promoting not only social justice but community involvement, Henderson said.[17]

---

[17] Hatcher, "Rural Faith Communities Play Anchoring Role." *Institute for Emerging Issues* (March 28, 2018), https://iei.ncsu.edu/2018/03/28/rural-faith-communities-as-anchor-institutions/.

When the rural small church is viewed as an anchor institution, a renewed appreciation and understanding of its unique role in the community is achieved. The church's self-narrative and definition of ministry success or fruitfulness need to take the responsibilities of an anchor institution seriously. A church in a city context may be able to sharply concentrate its goals for an outreach ministry, knowing that other nonprofits and agencies may already take care of other needs. Conversely, the rural small church must consider the health and vitality of the entire community, knowing that the church may be the only institution the community has for accessible social services.

When a rural church is seeking to discern God's giftedness, the needs of the community, and how to reach people for Jesus, they often don't have to look far to seek the expertise and resources of community leaders. The school principal, the mayor, the police chief, and the business owner are not strangers. They are our neighbors and perhaps our fellow congregants sitting in the next pew. When an opportunity (or a crisis, such as a natural disaster) arises, the small rural church can mobilize people and partnerships to make a God-sized difference in people's lives. In his interview with the Lewis Center, author Allen Stanton shared the story of a rural congregation that discovered how to match community assets, an unfinished church building, and community needs to reach young people for Jesus:

> *Evangelism is the ability and the practice of recognizing the kingdom of God, cultivating the kingdom of God, announcing the kingdom of God, and inviting the wider community to participate in that kingdom of God. This lines up with an asset-based community development approach that takes stock of the resources that are already in the community, recognizes how God is already at work, and then seeks to cultivate those assets and form partnerships.*
>
> *An example is my friend Tim, who is a pastor here in Tennessee. Tim's assets were a bunch of angry contractors in*

his community who didn't have the workforce they needed and a bunch of high school kids who weren't going to go to college but didn't know how to swing a hammer. So, he had two components that needed each other but were also in conflict with each other. Tim said, "This is a resource from the kingdom of God. God is up to something in this particular moment." Tim also had the shell of a building. So, Tim recognized that God had given these assets and he began cultivating them. He said to the contractors, "Look, you guys need employees. These youth need mentorship, not just for job skills but for their whole selves. So why don't we create a youth ministry where you mentor them?" Every Thursday night, they would have a devotion to talk about how God was at work in their world, to talk about how God does that work in these students' lives to help the students and the mentors grow in discipleship. And then they learn the job skills. They started doing the wiring, laying pavers outside, putting up walls. . . .Tim is creating a job pipeline. But he's changing the lives of the students and mentors, too. It's not just developing a workforce, it's also pouring into the whole lives of these people and saying, "You matter. Your work matters. Our community matters in the kingdom of God. And this is part of it." It's about the mission and the work and the outreach and how that's forming us for discipleship.[18]

You can see why it's so important to invest in the community by building relationships beyond the congregation and by building trust in the community. Trust is built over the years but can be lost instantly. In a time when demographic shifts (smaller families and the population shift to cities) and technological changes (Zoom, etc.) have combined with the sparse population of rural areas, folks are increasingly isolated. So, make the church available as a community-gathering location and create opportunities for people of the community to meet one another and the congregation. The gathering can be social, educational, health care (a vaccine clinic or

---

[18] Hatcher, "Rural Faith Communities Play Anchoring Role."

a blood drive), charity-based, or a creative project like the discipling and "hammer swinging" training in the example above. Just open the church's doors wide and *do* something!

Small Church in Towns

For purposes of this resource, when we refer to a "town," we are generally referring to a county seat or a population large enough to support a post office, school, and some local businesses. Small churches in towns need to identify a signature ministry. All churches have limited resources. Small churches have limited resources but are usually very scrappy and can do a lot of ministry with far fewer resources than many of the larger churches since they are nimble and flexible. Small town churches can make an even greater impact when they choose one—maybe two—signature ministries and do them really well. The church becomes well-known for this particular ministry in the community. Likewise, the ministry gains prominence within the community and would be sorely missed if it were no longer available.

The members of vital small churches in towns are usually well-connected and well-known in their communities. Local community leaders are often a part of the church and are great connectors between the entities. Their home, work, and church life are often very integrated.

In small towns, the church may be known for who attends. Affinity groups form within the church over the years. For instance, the church may be where most of the teachers attend or where a vast majority of the white-collar or blue-collar community people attend. The church may also have a certain shared theological perspective. Sometimes the church continues to have the reputation in the community for an attending affinity group when, in fact, the affinity group no longer attends.

Small Church in Cities

For purposes of this resource, when we refer to a "city," we are generally referring to a densely populated area or what one might refer to as a metropolitan area. There are multiple multistory buildings, public transportation, and most any resource is available.

A church's mission field may be just a few blocks in extremely densely populated areas with high-rises. The mission field may be a mile or two in less densely populated cities. City mission fields are often very unique. I (Kay) worked with a church that had two very distinct mission fields surrounding their church. On one side of their mission field was a large homeless population within a commercial area that included a large hospital system, among other businesses. The entrance to a neighborhood featuring million-dollar homes was on the opposite side, adjoining the church property and mission field.

In small-city churches, vital small churches typically have boutique or passion-based ministries. For example, they are the churches with incredible recovery ministries, or they run a ministry for families who have adopted children or desire to adopt children. Or, it is a church passionate about mission trips to Tanzania to help elevate local Tanzanian women from challenging backgrounds by giving them a chance to upskill and work towards a sustainable income. The city church might even attract and serve a particular generation living nearby because of their shared life stage and interests (i.e., widows and widowers who love to travel).

It's All Contextual

No matter a church's size, it's always important to understand your context and resources and then identify how best to leverage them to reach your context. Just like large churches don't operate the same as midsize or small churches, not all small churches operate alike. Rural churches operate differently from town churches.

Town churches are distinctly different from city churches. It's also important to always keep your finger on the pulse of your context and your resources because, at any point, any of those could change, and the church would need to pivot to continue to stay relevant, competent, and vital.

Team Questions

1. What is your ministry setting? City, town, or rural?

2. What are the unique characteristics, history, and needs of your context?

3. Drilling down in your context:

a. **If your church is rural**, how is your church serving as an anhor institution for your community? Does the majority of the population consider the church an anchor institution? How do you know? To test your hunches, consider surveying several dozen people that no one in the church knows. How might you improve the perception, services, and/or relationship with the community based on what you learned in the survey?

b. **If your church is a small church in a town setting**, what is your signature ministry? How is that signature ministry part of the fabric of the community? Would a great number of community members notice or be impacted if that ministry were to stop? How do you know? How many from the congregation are involved in the signature ministry? Is it the best use of resources (time, energy, gifts, skills, experience, dollars, facility) to provide the highest possible Kingdom impact? How do you know? What is an accurate way to measure?

c. **If your church is in an urban setting,** what is your unique ministry and/or affinity who gather to do ministry together? What kind of impact is the ministry making for those the ministry is touching? How are you measuring this effectiveness? In an urban area, word can spread quickly about something people are excited about. How are people talking about the ministry with others, bringing awareness and new people to the ministry?

SECTION

2

Simplified, Accountable Structure in the Small Church

CHAPTER FIVE

Stay in Your Lane

Uncle Joe declares, "It's that time!" Everyone rushes to the backdoor and out onto the back lawn. Thanksgiving is always held at Grandma Jones' house because she has the best backyard for THE game. For the past thirty-plus years, there has always been the family touch-football game after dinner in Grandma Jones' backyard. Some look forward to the game more than the turkey dinner and pumpkin pie. It's tradition!

The teams are always the same, too. It's the Joneses and Millers on one team and the Kellys and Proctors on the other. Even though Grandpa Jones has been gone for seven years, they still play by *his* rules. Grandma Jones is the scorekeeper and sometimes even takes over as the referee. Some might even say she shows favoritism toward the little kids when it comes to some of her calls.

The goalposts at one end are the two trees that Great-Grandpa Jones planted. The goalposts on the other end are the clothesline that Grandma and Great-Grandma Jones have hung their laundry on to dry for over five decades. Long gone are the days when Uncle Joe and Uncle Sam got to stand on the sideline and coach their respective teams. As Great-Aunt Sue, Great-Uncle George, Great-Uncle Martin, and others age, the coaches now have to put on their helmets and play as they coach and manage. But it doesn't matter. A great time is had by all! Does anybody really remember the score anyway?

The Work vs. the People

Much like family backyard football games, smaller schools provide students with more participation opportunities. In larger schools, students most often don't have the opportunity to play multiple sports. For example, those most gifted in basketball will likely not have the opportunity to also play tennis. Those gifted in track and field will likely not have the opportunity to also wrestle. Sometimes student populations in larger schools are so huge that even talented athletes still don't get to play on a team, or they spend most of the games on the bench. Only elite athletes are given the opportunity to play. Yet, in schools with smaller class sizes, a student can participate in multiple sports.

The same is true for small churches. There are all kinds of opportunities to participate. Some may even say there are too many "opportunities." Many different activities are offered, and the same few people run from one game to the next without knowing the ending score, let alone discerning if they even want to participate! There is just an expectation of participation.

In larger churches, we refer to "four lanes" of accountable leadership: governance, management, leadership, and ministry. Often, leaders have a difficult time staying in their respective lanes. Those elected to serve in the governance lanes often veer into the management lanes. Those in leadership may be tempted to park in the management lane. Those who are to serve in ministry end up stalled in the management lane due to excessive congestion. This leaves the most critical lane of ministry deserted and the mission of the church unrealized.

In healthy churches with over sixty engaged people, these four distinct lanes—operating with responsibility, authority, and accountability—all have different people. See the chart below to reference how the football metaphor plays out in the larger church ministry model. No matter what size church, the idea is to reserve as many disciples as possible to be teammates (serve in impactful ministry). Note that anyone leading a team (whether paid or unpaid) is in management and should be considered part of a staff team. Management is not hired to do the ministry. Those leading ministry teams are responsible for identifying the gifts, graces, and passions of disciples and recruiting them into areas of ministries that sync with those gifts, graces, and passions. The leaders then equip the disciples for ministry and deploy them to impact, nurture, disciple, and reach new people for Christ to transform communities and the world.

Position	Players	Functions	Metaphors
Ministry	Congregation	Serve in impactful ministry, disciples nurturing and developing disciples, reaching new people for Christ	Teammates, champions, athletes
Management	Staff/ Team Leaders	Identify, recruit, equip, and deploy disciples for ministry. Coordinate resources, disciples and ministries.	Assistant coaches and specialists
Leadership	Lead Pastor	Spiritual leader and shepherd. Supervise and evaluate staff. Align ministries, staffing, and resources to the vision and goals.	Head coach, quarterback, captain
Governance	Board	Stewardship, Generative work, Strategy, Hold Lead Pastor (and ministries) accountable to the vision and goals.	Commissioner, umpire, scorekeeper & cheerleader

In smaller churches, instead of different *people* being in different lanes of ministry, we have to think of the different lanes of work in the church. If no clear distinctions exist in the various types of work to be completed, the church leaders will likely not travel in all the lanes or see the distinction and value in the different kinds of work. The default lane is management, no matter what size the church is. The most important lanes are ministry and governance. Unfortunately, in most any size church, the governance lane almost always has grass growing up in the cracks of the asphalt because it is so seldom traveled. The ministry lane is greatly underutilized as our denomination has placed a high value on committee work and meetings rather than releasing people for the highest Kingdom impact work—ministry!

When churches fail to practice accountable leadership, ministries are often ineffective. Sure, there may be a lot of activity at the church (teammates running around on the field), but no one can remember the last time the football has seen the end zone and points were put up on the scoreboard (a new person came to know Christ or the community was transformed through the church's ministry). Another example is when a Church Council simply rubber stamps the same budget with the same line items and ministries year after year. In other words, no one is asking if the plays (ministries, events, programs) the coaches are calling are actually resulting in touchdowns (making and maturing disciples).

Of course, no one will fire Uncle Joe as the coach for the Thanksgiving Day family football game. But we all know that high school, college, or professional coaches will not keep their jobs long if their teams do not score any points! Yet, many churches never keep score or even consider the need to keep score. I (Kay) live in the Kansas City area. (Go, Chiefs!) Can you imagine Clark Hunt, the owner of the Kansas City Chiefs, not holding Coach Andy Reid accountable for identifying, recruiting, equipping, and deploying a winning football team? Do you think Andy Reid would keep his job for one minute if the Kansas City Chiefs never won a game? Jesus is the owner of the church. As leaders of the church, we are accountable to Christ for putting a winning team (maturing disciples who make disciples) on the field (out in the community) to score points (to reach new people and provide impactful ministries).

Many small church Leadership Boards struggle with trying to

do ministry, manage, and govern simultaneously. This would be like trying to simultaneously be the referee, cheerleader, special teams coach, and player. It is absolutely impossible to do all of these things at the same time. These roles are vitally important to the success of the team and the game, but no one person can do them all, especially at the same time. This is why it is highly suggested in mid-sized and larger churches that no one leading a ministry area (team leader) simultaneously serves on the Leadership Board. It is very difficult to separate those two areas of focus and responsibility. Therefore, the leader will weave out of their respective lane of accountable leadership and try to manage (call the plays, plan ministry) when they need to govern (keeping score, cheerleading, refereeing, leveraging assets to align to goals, strategic planning).

If the church struggles with having enough people to ensure each role has its own distinctive people, then at least the work needs to be recognized by its distinctive *lanes*. Instead of setting aside different people for different roles, be incredibly intentional on how each role is being lived out in the church. Management (ministry planning, ministry coordination) is not done at Leadership Board meetings. Day-to-day ministry is freed up by permission-giving tools created by the Leadership Board as they stay out of management. The Leadership Board does generative work, like bringing in the chamber of commerce president to share at the board meeting about the new business coming to town and how this business will reshape the community. This generative work provides an opportunity for the Leadership Board to realign its strategic plan (plays) and realign its assets (team players, coaches) so the church (team, franchise) can continue to be effective, relevant, and compelling (winning football team) in their ever-changing local context (league).

When working with one church new to the accountable leadership model, I (Kay) discovered that most of the Leadership

Board members were also ministry team leaders. Those poor leaders had such a difficult time staying out of the management lane! They spent fifteen minutes talking about how to handle the issue of getting people who used the facility to turn down the thermostat when they left. Another time, a Leadership Board spent ten minutes chatting about the community lunch menu and their personal favorite. The conversation stalled on macaroni and cheese for ten minutes. Yes, that's right! Ten leaders (plus me) wasted a total of 110 minutes of our lives (that we will never get back) talking about macaroni and cheese. No decision even needed to be made about the menu. They just went off on this wild tangent and no one noticed or called the group into accountability. Of course, they were shocked when I provided the feedback at the end of the meeting that they had actually spent that much time talking about macaroni and cheese. What a waste! And this is one very good reason why so many people (younger generations in particular) will not serve in church leadership roles.

There is Hope!

Once a Leadership Board and ministry team leaders are trained in accountable leadership and have the opportunity to practice the model, most leaders find it very refreshing. The model helps focus conversations and makes decision-making much easier and faster. Because time is being used more efficiently and leaders are being trusted to be responsible for their own work, the decisions made are much more missionally aligned, and the church is more effective in its purpose of making disciples. Accountable leadership is a complete change in leadership culture. It is important to remember that changing culture takes time. It will take some practice and time to live into the model, but once a church has fully leaned into it, the value in adopting it will be quite obvious.

Team Questions

1. What work lanes are currently functioning in your church? Which ones are not?

2. What are some initial first steps the leaders could take to start modeling accountable leadership?

3. How could identifying the work lanes and implementing accountable leadership benefit your church?

CHAPTER SIX

Structuring Leadership in the Small Church

It was a meeting like most church board meetings. You walked into the room, picked up your copy of the minutes and finances, and took a seat. The pastor opened in prayer. Then the reporting started—it seemed like it would never end. Endless reports about what had already been done were read directly from a report, word by word, that would become part of the minutes. If there were no real decisions to be made, it was more of a process for the proverbial "rubber stamp." No one was quite sure who really had a vote, so everyone voted, and obviously, therefore, everyone had a voice.

There was never a mention of how the church was aligning itself (or not) to the mission of disciple-making. There was no mention of annual goals and progress. No one had a clue if there were any baptisms or professions of faith. We were simply there to hear reports and rubber-stamp any decision brought before the group. Some left the meeting feeling like it was a big waste of time. We were just going through the motions. Any real conversations were conducted in the parking lot after the meeting. And the meetings have gone this way for decades—or more.

Does that sound like any church board meeting you have ever attended? If so, allow us to give you hope by offering another way, a more faithful and effective method to lead the church.

While polity differences exist from denomination to denomination, the United Methodist churches we know have traditionally been structured with four administrative committees. Those four committees include Finance, Trustees, Pastor-Parish Relations Committee (PPRC), and the Administrative Board/ Church Council. Each team functions separately. The interesting part is the difference from church to church in how the committees relate (or not) to one another and how they relate to the pastor (or not). Those differences denote how the structure functions and the chain of command. For most organizations, this is commonly demonstrated in an organizational chart.

When consulting with congregations, it is always a fun exercise to ask the church leaders to sketch their organizational chart. First, most churches have never really considered mapping their structure, let alone creating an actual chart on paper or virtually. Second, most times, a variety of charts are presented to us. Sometimes leaders report not even knowing where to start. In small churches, leaders sometimes throw up their hands and say, "Well, we are all members, so we all just get together and vote." We are often handed at least six to eight different and conflicting charts from the same church. No wonder we struggle with our current structure! We must have a common understanding of how each committee relates to the others, who is responsible for what, how we function together and separately, and how the pastor relates to each committee or team.

In addition to all the challenges mentioned above, another challenge is when a church finds itself with a huge number of positions to fill but a limited number of people to fill all the "slots." Once all the official administrative committees are filled—or perhaps partially filled—there is only a small number of people to fill the actual "doing of ministry" positions. We seem to place a higher emphasis on filling the administrative positions first, thus leaving a small percentage of leaders to with time and energy to guide and participate in ministries. This pattern is especially true in small churches where everyone must wear two or three—or maybe six or seven—leadership "hats."

By spending so much energy on administrative leadership committees, we tend to focus on our internal affairs more than on doing ministry to reach new people for Jesus Christ—our very mission! This practice is one of the many reasons we have an abundance of internally focused churches struggling to be vital and who are disconnected from their communities. Our legacy structures of multiple administrative committees were designed in the post-World War II era for a midsized congregation with 150-200 active members. Because of the cumbersome nature of operating in the structure created in the 1950s and '60s, more and more churches are moving to a leaner, streamlined, effective, and efficient structure. It is time to right-size your church's leadership and governance to match your current reality, culture, and the impact you want your congregation to make.

The United Methodist Church's 2016 *Book of Discipline (BOD)*, ¶ 247.2, provides a provision to structure your church uniquely for missional purposes:

> *The charge conference, the district superintendent, and the pastor shall organize and administer the pastoral charge and churches according to the policies and plans herein set forth. When the membership size, program scope, mission resources, or other circumstances so require, the charge conference may, in consultation with and upon the approval of the district superintendent, modify the organizational plans, provided that the provisions of ¶ 243 are observed.*[19]

---

[19] *The Book of Discipline of The United Methodist Church* 2016 (United Methodist Publishing House, 2016).

And ¶ 243 reads:

> *¶ 243. Primary Tasks—The local church shall be organized so that it can pursue its primary task and mission in the context of its own community—reaching out and receiving with joy all who will respond; encouraging people in their relationship with God and inviting them to commitment to God's love in Jesus Christ; providing opportunities for them to seek strengthening and growth in spiritual formation; and supporting them to live lovingly and justly in the power of the Holy Spirit as faithful disciples.*[20]

A church must still fulfill the requirements for the responsibilities of Finance (dollars), Trustees (property, assets, and legal affairs), and Pastor-Parish Relations (personnel), as well as the Church Council. However, fulfilling those responsibilities can be accomplished with more effective and efficient methods that reflect more modern systems and practices.

Because of the generalized wording in the *BOD* ¶ 247, a variety of ways have been created to streamline structure. There is no one way that is right or perfect. But we have walked alongside hundreds of congregations across the country to implement this, and we will share best practices based on the collection of those experiences. You will need to consider local context and values when establishing the new structure.

Our recommendation, whenever possible and as a best practice, is to do a pure, complete model of the simplified, accountable structure (SAS) that is fully outlined in our book, *Mission Possible 3+: A Simple Structure for Missional Effectiveness.*[21] Adopting this structure means the church must roll its four administrative committees into one single board of six to nine members (plus the

---

[20] *The Book of Discipline.*
[21] Kay L. Kotan and Phil Schroeder, *Mission Possible 3+: A Simple Structure for Missional Effectiveness* (Market Square Publishing, June 2021).

pastor acting in an executive capacity). Technically, the Trustees, Finance Committee, and PPRC still exist, but they exist as one combined board taking on all the roles, responsibilities, and authority of the four committees as a single administrative committee we refer to as the Leadership Board.

Leadership Board = Council + Trustees + Past-Parish Relations + Finance

Combining these different committee functions into a single Leadership Board creates some wonderful benefits:

- Unleashes lay leaders from the committee room to make disciples of Jesus.

- Allows a small church to minimize administration to maximize ministry.

- Focuses on the mission field instead of "turf wars" from different committees, such as the Trustees and Finance Committees tussling over some assets.

- Aligns disciples and leverages resources to fulfill your ministry goals as you live into God's preferred future for your church.

- Reduces bureaucracy, redundancy, and meetings.

- Increases efficiency, decision-making and visioning becomes nimbler and more flexible.

- Ministry teams come together for a specific purpose (i.e., VBS) and disband when finished. No long-standing committees are required for short-term defined ministries.

Of course, fewer people making decisions is NOT the goal of moving to a simplified, accountable leadership structure. The goal of any change in structure must ultimately be about successfully implementing the Christ-centered mission of the congregation to make disciples more effectively. You need a governing and strategic structure to help manifest this holy mission.

In the small church, there is also the added benefit of not having to beg one leader to serve on three different committees just to submit your charge conference paperwork. In this way, a simplified structure is often an acknowledgment of reality. Please note: district superintendents have rejected applications from congregations seeking to move toward a single Leadership Board to sideline critics of the pastor. Simplifying your structure is not about consolidating power. It is about making the congregation's decision-making nimbler and unleashing laity for more ministry and impact! This is yet another reason why simplifying structure and accountable leadership go hand in hand.

How to Structure

First, a common mistake in describing a simplified, accountable structure is to say that "we got rid of all of our committees." Actually, all your administrative committees still exist, and, in their combined form, all their responsibilities constitute the authority of the new Leadership Board. In other words, the Leadership Board *is* the Finance Committee, *is* the Pastor-Parish Committee, *is* the Trustees, and *is* the Church Council. Nothing in the *Book of Discipline* is ignored or removed. Instead, the functions, roles, and responsibilities of each of the constituent committees are placed upon your new consolidated Leadership Board. This means that the Leadership Board conforms to the qualifications of all four administrative committees simultaneously. The Leadership Board must have at least one-third men and one-third women to fit the Trustees' requirements. No household members of pastors or staff are allowed, and spouses cannot serve on the board together in deference to the PPRC rules. Only professing members may serve.

Take every requirement from the *Discipline* for each included committee (Church Council, Finance, PPRC, and Trustees) and apply it to the Leadership Board. If a conflict is noticed, take the more stringent requirement as a matter of integrity.

To move into the most simplified structure, you will need six to nine members, plus the pastor. Because nine is the standard-sized committee required by the *Book of Discipline* for Trustees, Finance, and SPRC, this is the recommended size for a simplified structure. We offer the option of six leaders for the smallest churches because that number fulfills the minimal *Book of Discipline* requirements while also offering the smallest church a more streamlined approach. The other official committee that will need to be elected by the charge conference is the Nominations Committee. (There is more about the Nominations Committee later in this chapter. And again, for even more information, refer to *Mission Possible 3+*.)

Organizational Charts

You will find an example of the recommended organizational chart for smaller churches that outlines a simplified structure with accountable leadership below. This chart illustrates clear lines of authority, responsibility, and accountability (aka accountable leadership, see Chapter 3). It provides clarity for who reports to who and the role of each. You will notice some differences between this chart and the one that follows, which is for a mid-sized church.

First, some ministry team leaders in the smaller church will "report to" or be held accountable to the board, not the pastor. These leaders and teams in mid-sized and larger churches should always be under the pastor's leadership. However, since the role of the pastor in smaller congregations is very contextual, running a spectrum from effectively serving as a quarter-time chaplain to a role more akin to that of an executive director, there needs to be some contextual flexibility. Most importantly, don't approve a ministry team without also clearly—and in writing—stating who the leader is and to whom (the Leadership Board chair, the pastor, or another designee) the ministry team leader is accountable. We offer more guidance on maintaining roles in Chapter 5, "Stay in Your Lane." This is where working with a certified SAS coach (coach-trained and certified by the authors to work with church leaders and churches in this model) can be extremely helpful.

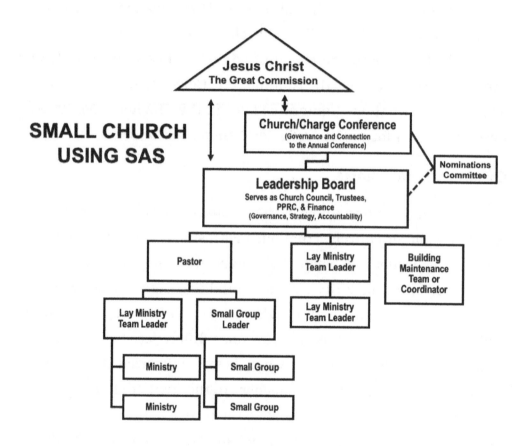

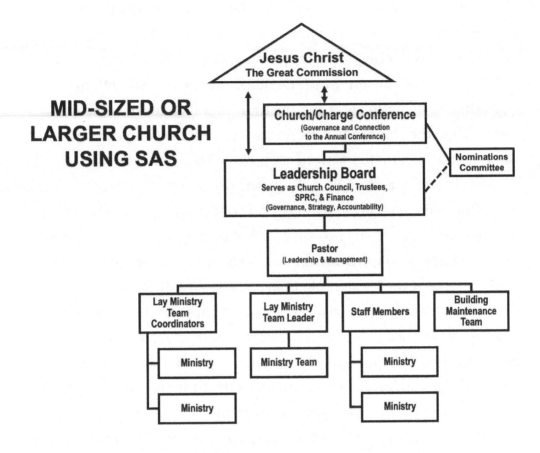

Organizing the Initial Leadership Board

The charge conference will elect the chair of the Leadership Board (we recommend they be nominated by the Nominations Committee one year at a time). To ensure alignment, good communication flow, and role clarity, it is recommended that the Leadership Board member elected as the Leadership Board chair also be elected as the trustee chair at the board's initial meeting each January (there are legal and disciplinary rules that require this to be a separate vote of the board itself).

Likewise, we recommend the Leadership Board chair be named by the Nominations Committee as the Staff/Pastor-Parish Relations liaison to the district superintendent. This recommendation comes from some difficult experiences when the Leadership Board chair was not the district superintendent's contact. As a DS, I (Blake) have gotten conflicting requests from a Leadership Board chair and a separate PPRC liaison, which muddied the waters, disciplinary speaking. Information was coming in from someone on the board rather than the chair, and information was not necessarily being shared or disseminated with the rest of the board members.

In yet another example, I (Kay) was working with a church where the PPRC liaison received the pastoral consultation form from the district office, pulled in two other PPRC "reps" to complete the form, and submitted it to the DS without any conversation or consultation with the rest of the Leadership Board, who had a different recommendation for the pastoral appointment than the PPRC liaison and her cohort had reported. Therefore, it is deemed a best practice for all outside coordination or correspondence to be done through the board chair, serving in their capacity as the PPRC chair. And official actions of the board must have the input and vote of the entire board.

We recommend that the Nominations Committee report to the charge conference and make it clear that the Leadership Board chair fulfills all the presidential functions, and that your Leadership Board make it a custom to elect the Leadership Board chair to be the chair of the Trustees. In addition to electing the chair of Trustees, the Leadership Board will also need to select a secretary of the board of Trustees from its membership. While notetaking duties may be passed around, the roles of trustee chair and trustee secretary have legal implications, especially if the congregation buys property or is registered with your state's Secretary of State as a nonprofit corporation.

The Nominations Committee can use notations to show particular roles of committees for individual members, such as the lay leader or the lay member of the annual conference (see the chart below). Note that youth under eighteen cannot serve on the Board of Trustees. The Leadership Board must also comply with the *Discipline's* Board of Trustees requirement that at least one-third of the members be men and at least one-third be women. Note: This does not preclude persons under eighteen from serving on the Leadership Board. It only means that when a vote with legal implications is taken, any member of the Leadership Board under eighteen must be recused from the vote.

To comply with the *BOD* and to keep the team fresh and accountable, you will still need to place members into three classes (i.e., Class of 2024, Class of 2025, Class of 2026). Once the membership of the new Leadership Board is decided, the Committee on Nominations and Leadership Development will need to divide the initial group into three classes to begin a series of rotations, with two or three people in each class, depending on whether the board is composed of six or nine members.

A WORD OF ADVICE AND CAUTION:

We have seen the simplified structure quickly go off track when congregations, fearful of losing the wisdom of the initial class of leaders, decide to ignore the rotating class system and either push back rotation dates or immediately "re-up" those who served only one year for another term. Don't fall into the trap of thinking the church "can't do without" a certain leader on the board. Those previous leaders can also be brought into a work team for their historical perspective or expertise if needed. It's not like they are leaving the church. Succession classes are important for your Leadership Board's accountability, and even in the small church, you need to practice rotation of leaders even if you must, for the sake of numbers, rotate a person back through for an additional term.

With classes in place, one-third of the board will then rotate off each year, and new people will be seated. This rotation allows for continuity, historical preservation, and the important work of onboarding and equipping new leaders each year.

Finally, take the time to carefully discern your structure for your context. As stated above, the *Book of Discipline* requirements and qualifications for the committees apply to your new Leadership Board, which means that your Nominations Committee will be flipping through multiple sections of the *Book of Discipline.* Structure by photocopy is not enough preparation. Your Nominations Committee will need to fully understand and be able to communicate the mechanics of your new structure.

Example of a Leadership Board Roster
(6-9 Elected Board Members in the Small Church)

Class of 2024
John Jones, T/F/PPR
Carol Clark, T/F/PPR/LM
Yolanda Youngperson (under 18 youth member), F/PPR/Y

Class of 2025
Sue Smith, T/F/PPR
David Dent, T/F/PPR
Maria Martínez, T/F/PPR

Class of 2026
Jennifer Jackson, T/F/PPR/C/LL
Ben Black, T/F/PPR
Larry Lewis, T/F/PPR

The appointed pastor is ex officio, serving with a vote only in matters defined in the Book of Discipline.

Key

T – Trustee	C – Chair of the Board
F – Finance	PPR – Pastor-Parish Relations
LL – Lay Leader	
Y – Youth Member (if under 18, cannot serve as a trustee)	
LM – Lay Member to Annual Conference	

Building Maintenance is Different than the Board of Trustees

Let us take a moment and talk specifically about the Board of Trustees and building maintenance—another area where churches often get tripped up when moving to the simplified structure. In many churches, members of the Board of Trustees have been tapped, practiced, or labeled as those who perform the actual hands-on work on the building and grounds. They maintain the grounds, change the light bulbs in the sanctuary, and fix the running toilet. We refer to this kind of work as "tool-belt work." The trustees also take care of the fiduciary responsibilities (such as property insurance, facility policies, lease agreements, filing bylaws, and articles of incorporation with the state). We refer to this type of work as "briefcase work."

In most cases, the majority of the trustee committee's time is spent on building and parsonage repairs and maintenance. By and large, these trustees have become great stewards of the facilities, and we thank God for these people.

In the traditional committee-driven structure, the Board of Trustees is given the authority and responsibility to oversee and maintain the property and conduct the church's legal affairs. The committee is given the responsibility, but nowhere does it state an expectation that the members of the Board of Trustees must personally do the toolbelt work of building maintenance. This shift just evolved over time, and the lines became blurred. Facility management became the most consuming and demanding of the trustees' time and attention, causing this shift from a fiduciary/governing focus to one of management.

As discussed in Chapter 5, "Stay in Your Lane," this combination of fiduciary governance and maintenance/management work causes whiplash in swerving back and forth between the governance, management, and ministry lanes. In the traditional model of multiple committees, trustees weren't sure if they needed to bring their briefcases or toolbelt to meetings! Should they bring their work gloves, or was this a "put on your tie" kind of meeting? The Committee on Nominations wasn't sure if they were looking for disciples with gifts in building and grounds maintenance or legal and insurance expertise. Separating these two distinct, separate functions *regardless of church structure* is a best practice to ensure members understand which lane this ministry is meant to be driven in.

Maintenance needs obviously do not go away in the simplified model. Our church property still needs to be maintained. Our recommendation and experience as a best practice are to have a member or even a ministry team assigned to do building maintenance. Using written and approved guiding principles, give this person or team the authority and responsibility to care for repairs and maintenance within healthy parameters set by the Leadership Board, such as spending limits, rules on when bids are needed, and when to call a professional. This practice provides permission for the person or team to proceed with building maintenance without being bogged down in the administrative and fiduciary responsibilities and meetings now being handled by the Leadership Board, such as handling matters like the child protection policy or insurance.

Keep a Separate Nominations Committee and Leadership Development

A separate, independent Nominations Committee, with the pastor as chair, is also required by the *Book of Discipline.* The Committee on Nominations and Leadership Development nominates members of only two committees: the Leadership Board and the Nominations Committee itself. For the most part, these will be the only two standing committees with governance responsibility.

The *BOD* does not allow the duties of the Nominations Committee to be rolled into the new simplified Leadership Board, so it will continue to exist and serve as an independent body. The Committee on Nominations and Leadership Development is to have three to nine members, not including the pastor, who is the chair of the committee, plus the lay leader. Members are placed in three classes. For the small church, you can have six or even three members. Divide the total into three equal classes. If there are six members, have two in each of the three classes; if there are three members, put each of them into a separate class.

Ministry teams are created and discontinued as needed to accomplish the goals. There is no need for standing teams in name only (like we practiced in the traditional structure model) whose membership is elected as an annual slate proposed by the Nominations Committee. For example, there is no longer a standing Children's Education Committee. Instead, if the church decides Vacation Bible School (VBS) aligns with its goals, the pastor (or other identified leader) identifies, recruits, and equips a leader with the gifts and passions to lead a VBS Ministry Team three to four months prior to VBS. This ministry team leader then pulls together the ministry team to implement VBS based on the goals, desired outcome, and some simple trackable measurements outlined by the pastor (or other identified leader) based on the Accountable Leadership Cycle. At the conclusion of VBS, the VBS Ministry Team evaluates VBS against the goals, desired outcomes, and trackable measurements. The VBS Ministry Team then disbands as their work is finished. (Refer to Chapter 3 for a reminder on accountable leadership and the Accountable Leadership Cycle.)

In very small churches with few members, it is often difficult to organize the Nominating Committee due to sheer numbers, particularly if you want to get a maxed-out committee of nine members. We have often observed that, since spouses can't serve together on the Leadership Board, they may be helpful to have on the

Nominations Committee. If this is your practice, please be careful that the board and the system are not being insular and self-focused. The Nominations Committee must always consider who is being left out of leadership and encourage new folks who show potential to become church leaders.

Small-Church Structuring Summary

This chapter's steps and suggestions for structure changes might feel foreign or even difficult—especially if this is your first introduction to a simplified, accountable structure. We can assure you it only feels this way because any type of change most always feels overwhelming in the beginning. Changing structure and leadership models is no different. However, we find that churches (no matter the size) that fully embrace simplified, accountable structure most always find themselves within a year feeling unencumbered by meetings, waiting for committee decisions, more nimble and flexible, and much more missionally focused. It just takes some time to get used to the new permission-giving structure.

Team Questions

1. Is your church's current structure traditional or simplified? How effective is your current leadership structure? What measurements would you use to gauge how effectively it functions?

2. Ask each team member to sketch the current organizational structure as it currently functions for information and communication flow and authority and decision-making. Compare each other's sketches. What insights did you gain from this exercise?

3. What steps might the leaders consider to simplify the structure to free up more people for ministry, make decision-making more efficient, and make resources more missionally aligned?

4. How do the trustees' toolbelt and briefcase work currently function? What improvements can be made? How can the people who tend to the maintenance of the facility and grounds be given permission and authority to go about their ministry without having to attend meetings or be fiduciary officers?

CHAPTER SEVEN
The Leadership Board at Work

Keeping the work of the Leadership Board simple and focused will be key in the small church. The principles in this chapter are designed to bring some consistency and clarity to everyone's roles and responsibilities while also smoothing over roadblocks and time-wasting, extra meetings that get in the way of the board simply making a decision. While the steps may seem more "business-like" than your small church is accustomed to, the tools are actually designed to keep things simple and mission-focused. In our book *Impact! Reclaiming the Call of Lay Ministry,* we explain that today's leaders expect and hope to make a real difference in the world and don't want to waste time waiting for outdated church committees to act:

> *If the process of moving from ministry idea to ministry implementation is too cumbersome, today's leaders will opt out. Gone are the days where a church can take four to six months running decisions through multiple committees to make critical decisions. Our world works at a much quicker pace today, and we are living in a post-Christendom culture [the church is no longer the center or driver of culture] that simply won't wait for the church to catch up. Leaders are looking to work within a governance process where real and greater IMPACT can be experienced routinely.*

Modern leaders desire the opportunity to [quickly and efficiently] mobilize fellow laity for missional IMPACT. That is IMPACT that ties directly to the mission and vision of the church. Leaders want to connect the dots of their ministry tied directly to the big picture of the church's purpose. Today's leaders, especially Millennials, desire the opportunity to make a real difference in the community, not fill a slot on a denominational form. Modern leaders will not invest their gifts, time and energy in activities that do not make a real difference. They desire effective and efficient God-sized IMPACT! [22]

As discussed in Chapter 5, "Stay in Your Lane," it is important not to veer into the management lane even when your leaders might have management responsibilities due to the limited number of people available. When folks show up to a Leadership Board meeting, they need to have their "board member" hats on and lay aside all the church member hats they usually carry around.

The Agenda is Essential

To stay focused and keep the work of the Leadership Board in the proper governance lane, starting with a functional agenda that supports this kind of work is essential. The traditional agenda consisting of old business, new business, and the reading of multiple reports will not separate your work and will surely veer you right into a traffic jam in the management and ministry lanes. Avoid this at all costs!

Instead, we recommend the following agenda, which (with practice) can be completed in about ninety minutes when leading in the simplified, accountable structure identified in Chapters 3 and 6. The Leadership Board chair leads the meetings.

---

[22] Kay Kotan and Blake Bradford, *Impact! Reclaiming the Call of Lay Ministry* (Market Square Publishing, May 2018), 110-111.

> **Opening Prayer**
>
> **Spiritual Formation**
>
> **Leadership Development**
>
> **Consent Calendar Items**
>
> **Fiduciary Work**
>
> **Missional Accountability Work**
>
> **Strategic and Planning Work**
>
> **Pressing Issues/Problem-Solving**
>
> **Executive Session (PPRC)**
>
> **Communication**
>
> **Closing Prayer**

Let's break down each item in the agenda to clarify each item, its purpose, timeframe, and who leads each.

Opening & Closing Prayer

Each leader on the Leadership Board will take a turn leading the opening and closing prayer. While the pastor is in the rotation, the pastor is not the sole person to lead prayer at the church. For laity to be comfortable when the time comes to pray outside the church, they must first be comfortable praying inside the church with their peers. To simplify the rotation, we suggest the one who is offering spiritual formation lead the opening prayer and the one who is offering leadership development lead the closing prayer.

Spiritual Formation

As spiritual leaders of the church, the Leadership Board models healthy, mature spiritual practices by starting the gathering of leaders with a time of spiritual formation. Rather than a Leadership Board member pulling something off the internet the night before the meeting, it is recommended that the spiritual formation is intentionally planned and based on where the Leadership Board has discerned it would be helpful to grow spiritually as leaders to live more faithfully into God's preferred future for the church. It might be one resource, topic, or book of the Bible that is used for a prolonged period of time. Every member of the Leadership Board takes their turn in leading spiritual formation.

Leadership Development

Again, as church leaders, the Leadership Board members are responsible for leading the church in its mission to make disciples. Given that responsibility, the leadership needs to take the time to discern what areas of focus, topics, or learning gaps would better equip them for their leadership role and responsibilities. This could be several topics or resources or one topic or resource that is used for an entire year. The idea is that it is intentional and purposeful. Every leader takes their turn in leading the leadership development time.

These first three items on the agenda (opening prayer, spiritual formation, and leadership development) are intended to take about thirty minutes. They are first on the agenda intentionally. First, it is critically important to develop and invest in leaders. Second, if this development time were last on the agenda, Leadership Boards would never get to them! Third, it helps center the leaders, ground them in their work, and remind them why the church exists.

Packet & Consent Calendar Items

The Leadership Board chair and pastor work collaboratively to pull together the packet and agenda. Ultimately the board chair is responsible. The packet needs to go out to the members of the Leadership Board about a week before the meeting. Ideally, the packet is shared electronically. The packet contains the following: minutes of the previous meeting, financial report, consent calendar/ agenda, new people report, goal report, and supporting documents for any other agenda-related items. The items placed on the consent calendar (aka consent agenda) should be clearly indicated in the packet and on the agenda.

When the Leadership Board gets to the consent calendar items on the agenda, the chair announces such and asks for a motion to approve the consent calendar items as presented in the packet. If there is a first and second motion, the chair calls for a vote. If the vote passes, the Leadership Board has approved everything on the consent calendar simultaneously instead of voting on each item separately. Efficiency at its best! Items can be removed from the consent calendar using the same process or another as identified in the guiding principles (see "guiding principles" later in this chapter). Typically, this takes just a minute or two on the agenda unless items are removed from the consent calendar and handled individually.

Fiduciary Work

This part of the agenda covers anything related to the facility, land, other assets, or financials (not already covered on the consent calendar). This would be related to items that fall outside the building maintenance team and guiding principles. In other words, this should not turn into a time to discuss light bulbs and carpet bids. This is a time to consider buying or selling property, building remodels, capital expenditure projects, building insurance, or the church's 501(c)(3) status, etc. Likely, items in this category will not be on the agenda every board meeting. That's okay. Just note there is no business to discuss on the agenda and skip it. There is no need to create something for the agenda topic.

Missional Accountability

This part of the agenda is two-fold: new people and ministry goals. We will start with the topic of reaching new people for Christ. Since the church exists to make disciple-making disciples who transform the world, it's imperative to check in on our progress. Having this mission on the agenda reminds us of our purpose and holds us accountable. Too often, we hold meeting after meeting and never address our progress toward our mission/purpose. Before we know it, a decade has passed, the church has fallen into decline, and not once have we had the conversation in a Leadership Board meeting about our accountability to Christ and our responsibility to the Great Commission.

The pastor is the primary one who reports on "new people." While in larger churches, a dashboard report might be created and included in the packet to communicate the number of new guests or new people engaged in the life of the church, in small churches, the report typically includes new people's names and any information learned about the guests. Each church needs to decide what kind of information they feel is the most appropriate in their context to help them know if new people are relating to the congregation and coming to know Christ due to the church's ministry. Whatever gauge the Leadership Board decides to use, use it consistently and look for trends of health and vitality. Note: Coming to know Christ does not necessarily result in Sunday morning worship attendance. Keep this in mind when determining the best gauge for your leaders to gauge missional effectiveness. If there is little or no impact, the Leadership Board will then need to address what course correction needs to be made so that the church can adjust and align with its mission of making disciples.

Most often, this takes five minutes or less. The exception will be if there needs to be an extended conversation because no impact has been made, and a course-correction conversation is needed. If this is the case, allow fifteen minutes or more to discuss or move this to the strategic or generative part of the agenda. Celebrate how the ministries engage new people in the community and build new relationships. Likewise, hold one another accountable to have the tough conversations if no impact is being made.

The second part of missional accountability involves reporting on the progression of the goals set for the year. Small churches may not have a formal strategic ministry-planning process to set annual goals, but hopefully, there are one or two key items the church is focusing on in any given year to become more vital and result in more Kingdom impact. Most often, this responsibility and reporting come from the pastor, but depending on the kind of pastoral appointment the church has, the responsibility for the goals may shift. For example, if there is only a quarter-time pastoral appointment, this may need to be shared with the board chair or a layperson who leads the ministry. Just be careful not to veer into management during this review. This is where there is the greatest danger for lane departure, so proceed with caution!

The purpose of the review is to ensure the focus that the leaders established as a priority for the year (i.e., goals) is being accomplished and the church is living out the mission of making disciples (which the goal should be focused on). The monthly review holds the leaders of the church's ministries (lay and clergy) accountable to the congregation's goals. A simple report—even just a copy of an email—can be included in the packet to help everyone stay on track for the ministry's goals. If the pastor is full-time, the conversation about particular ministries should be very limited, if at all. If the pastor is part-time (especially one-fourth time), more time and focus will need to be spent in this area or delegated to someone who provides an overview and answers questions.

The time allotted for this conversation depends on the number of goals the church has set and if progress is being made. If progress is being made, just a few minutes may be spent for clarification or celebration. If there is little to no goal-accomplishment progress, more time needs to be allotted for conversation to figure out why progress is stalled. This is an accountability conversation and is often new and even awkward for some congregations—especially for family-sized congregations. Check out this video of an accountability session in a board meeting for some assistance:

kaykotan.com/sas-accountability

Strategic & Planning Work

Typically, this is a whole new area of work for a Leadership Board. Because most Leadership Board meetings (or Church Councils in traditional structure) have been report-driven and not missionally driven, this is a huge shift for most Leadership Boards. Intentional planning and strategic work cause leaders to stare mission accountability squarely in the face and take responsibility for it.

The strategic work of the Leadership Board helps ensure that all resources are aligned and leveraged to their highest potential of making disciples. It pushes the leadership to maintain focus on their purpose and progress and make any necessary shifts as needed.

If strategic work is a new concept, generative work is downright foreign to most Leadership Boards. Yes, first, we need to accept that the Leadership Board is *generating* work, not just reacting to the items placed before them by others. That concept in itself is new to many Leadership Boards. Secondly, generative work is focused on the people in the community who have yet to know Jesus, not the congregation members who already have a relationship with Jesus. Third, most generative work consists of discerning where the Holy

Spirit is already at work in our community and how we can join for even more God-size impact rather than reading a report to one another about a ministry that has already happened. Think about the generative work as your lighthouse work (shining twenty-four miles out in a 360-degree parameter), whereas the previous agenda items are more of the headlight work (250 feet ahead in one direction) and even tail light work (reporting on past events).

Here are some examples of generative work for Leadership Boards:

- The only local grocery store in town is closing, and the closest grocery store will now be eighteen miles away. The community is concerned about the impact of this closing. A church two counties away encountered the same concern when their local grocery store closed. That church's pastor was invited to share with the Leadership Board how their church led a community effort to bridge the gap of this forthcoming food desert. This connection will provide the Leadership Board with insights and possibilities on how the church might be called to respond. Perhaps this is a time for the board to begin imagining a relational ministry that builds on and coordinates the existing assets of the larger community.

- Another example is a commercial farming corporation buying up a bunch of land in a rural church mission field. Since many of the congregants are farmers or descendants of farmers, they are concerned about what this might mean for their community, their personal livelihood, and the future generations of their mission field. The board chair invites the area representative of the Farm Service Agency (FSA) to present information to the board about this recent development, answer questions, and provide insights as to how this will affect the community. Again, this allows the Leadership Board to get out in front of the coming changes so that they can lead the church effectively, be advocates for the community, and determine how to appropriately respond to the changing landscape of their community.

- A third example of generative work is to conduct an intensive review of the community's demographics, including the top mosaic groups and segments. The Leadership Board would then identify a targeted mosaic segment they discern the church is called to reach. This strategic work would then inform what type of ministries would need to be planned for the ministry team leaders/coordinators. This approach simplifies and helps focus the ministry approach, which allows the church to be much more effective.

This strategic and generative work is what we refer to as the Leadership Board's balcony view (lighthouse). This high-altitude work requires peering outside the church with an intentional missional focus—a far stretch from the normal Church Council's routine of receiving reports and rubber-stamping. If a Leadership Board is truly missionally focused and practicing accountable leadership, more of the agenda and conversation will be focused on the community and those who are not yet a part of the congregation rather than the already-gathered congregation.

Since this is such a new type of leadership and conversation, many Leadership Boards simply skip this part of the agenda. Do NOT do this! The strategic and generative portion of the agenda is the most critical to cause the necessary shift in leadership culture toward more accountable leadership. Plan on spending a minimum of fifteen to twenty minutes of your agenda in this area. Move towards spending one-third of your agenda on this topic.

The chair facilitates the conversations for this part of the agenda, but this is where all members of the Leadership Board are expected to participate.

Pressing Issues/Problem-Solving

Most Leadership Boards and Church Councils spend the majority of their time (outside of reports) on pressing issues and problem-solving. For example, in the traditional structure when church councils typically took on a management role, there were conversations concerning the choice of paint colors, lawn care bids, and approving a new ministry. In the SAS model, the Leadership Board will want to move towards this being a more and more limited portion of your agenda. Once your guiding principles are in place and your Leadership Board becomes more governance-focused and less management-leaning, it will be much easier to keep this area of discussion at a minimum. While this area can't be eliminated, the more ministry team leaders/coordinators are empowered with permission and healthy boundaries through the guiding principles, the less pressing issues and problem-solving there are for the Leadership Board to address.

The Leadership Board chair will facilitate this conversation. Often the best result is to assign a workgroup or a specific person to figure out a solution, or provide a few options, and then the board can decide how it wants to conclude the matter, such as discussing options at the next meeting, approving or providing concurrence of a particular option by email or text, or providing some deadline for a workgroup to handle the matter and report back. Try to keep this part of the agenda less than ten minutes if at all possible.

Executive Session (Pastor-Parish Relations Work)

The work of the Pastor-Parish Relations Committee (PPRC) is required to be confidential, according to the United Methodist *Book of Discipline.* Just like in most businesses, personnel work in the church is confidential. The Leadership Board should include some time for the pastor and the board to engage in the relational work of support and mutual accountability. When there is Pastor-Parish business for the Leadership Board, move into executive session, in which any guests (anyone not officially voted into membership on the Leadership Board, plus the pastor) should be excused and minutes taken separately. During this time, the board members and the pastor should commit to sharing honestly, respectfully, and in the spirit of Christian love. Don't let "polite silence" get in the way of open communication.

Conversely, don't think of this segment of the agenda as "complaint time." The board and pastor are a team and should approach challenges and opportunities as a team, seeking God's reconciliation and mission. We have shared more about how the board and pastor should collaborate and communicate later in this chapter in the section about a Leadership Board Covenant.

Communication

Many leaders have shared that this simple reminder on the agenda has been such a game-changer for Leadership Boards and their congregations. Even in a small church, folks often complain that communication needs to be improved. As fewer people are involved in administrative leadership (shifting from Church Council to simplified, accountable leadership), communication needs to be ramped up. As the meeting is coming to an end, this "communication" agenda item is a time to ask ourselves, as leaders, what decisions were made at this meeting. First, identifying those decisions ensures the decisions are noted in the meeting minutes. Second, it ensures all the leaders hear the decisions again as a reminder, so there is a unified leadership voice. Third, it provides the opportunity for the Leadership Board to make decisions about how to *communicate* those decisions. Follow these communications steps at the end of each meetings to ensure a great communication strategy:

- What decisions have been made during our meeting?
- What is the messaging about each decision made?
- Who is the message carrier?
- How will the message be communicated?
- When should the message be communicated?

Maybe an email needs to be sent to the congregation after every board meeting, or a board member can verbally share during the announcement time in worship or at the monthly potluck.

Guiding Principles

Guiding principles are a set of policies and procedures (operational manual) that allow the church's ministry to function on a day-to-day basis within healthy boundaries and without the Leadership Board's engagement. Guiding principles keep the Leadership Board from managing and the pastor and ministry leaders from micromanaging. These principles are permission-giving processes, procedures, and strategies that protect the overall health and well-being of the church. Guiding principles allow for more effective decision-making by making macro decisions once rather than micro decisions repeatedly and continuously. Guiding principles free up the "decision bottleneck" that the old Church Council structure ultimately created and empower the pastor and ministry team leaders with authority to match their responsibilities and accountability.

Most churches start with a blank piece of paper in creating their guiding principles. While all of us have our United Methodist Church's *Book of Discipline (BOD)* to guide and direct us, there is certainly a need for local policies and procedures. Guiding principles complement the *BOD*—not replace the *BOD*. They might also further clarify the *BOD* in the local context.

Think of the guiding principles as a living, breathing document. Because our environment (people, ministries, community, etc.) changes constantly, guiding principles must grow and adapt as needed. Some churches might have existing policies or procedures that will be adopted or adapted for the guiding principles. A church might also refer to policies and procedures (i.e., employee manual, facility usage guide) in the guiding principles as a reference to their acceptance, knowledge of them or make them a separate section of the guiding principles. Some church leaders have appreciated having all of these "policies and procedures" in one place or document. Because of the organic nature of guiding principles, we highly recommend they be offered digitally as an open resource easily accessed by paid and unpaid staff and ministry team leaders.

Allow us to offer a filter for your Leadership Board's consideration. Every time the Leadership Board makes a decision, ask yourself if there could be a guiding principle established or modified that would have allowed the decision to be made earlier by the pastor, staff, or ministry team leader or without the Leadership Board's intervention. We are not suggesting that there needs to be a guiding principle for everything. Yet, many times, we could allow for a more natural and timely flow of ministry and day-to-day operations if the Leadership Board could grant more permission within guidelines through a guiding principle. Creating a permission-giving culture for staff and ministry team leaders provides a healthier environment for people to engage in their ministries when coupled with accountability throughout.

Furthermore, in a small church context, oftentimes, verbal permission is provided rather than written. Unfortunately, that does not always get communicated well or timely when a new person comes along or a new pastor is appointed. Furthermore, it is not always repeated or practiced consistently since it is not documented. This ambiguity leaves the new person at an incredible disadvantage. Documenting these operating procedures is more efficient and effective and saves time and confusion. The new person doesn't feel like they have to ask the "family" for permission or directions every time they turn around to do something new. The information is recorded and accessible to everyone.

A sample of guiding principles can be found in the resource section at the end of this book.

The Leadership Covenant

In addition to guiding principles, which sets out the authority and operational permission-giving from the board, we also recommend that the Leadership Board use a covenant to clarify how the board will lead, how they will do their work together, and what expectations the board members place on themselves and each other.

Each year with a few members rolling off the Leadership Board and a few new ones coming on, a new leadership covenant is created for the work ahead. We suggest that each member of the Leadership Board physically sign the covenant each year with an ink pen. This annual ritual helps leaders better grasp the commitment and promise they are making to one another, which is reflected through the words in the document.

This written covenant is a sacred agreement with God and other Leadership Board members that defines the expectations of leaders and a code of conduct upon which each Leadership Board member agrees. It speaks to how we will work together, collaborate with one another as a "team," and treat each other. Without a covenant, there will most likely be ambiguity.

A healthy team covenants together, and expectations are known and agreed upon before the work begins. In Kay's consulting, she always suggests the covenant start from scratch each year. The previous Leadership Board would not want to impose last year's covenant on the current Leadership Board. Of course, it can be used as a template, but copying last year's over to this year's takes away from its sacredness, the opportunity for new leaders to weigh in on its content, and the exercise of a fresh start and perspective each year. Once the covenant is agreed upon and put into writing, have each board member sign the covenant. This signing is a sacred time and practice, so approach it as such.

I (Kay) am often asked for a copy or a sample of a leadership covenant. I hesitate to offer one as I see too many times that churches will sidestep the journey through the important process and discernment. It is important that leaders create a covenant they can "own" and articulate in their words so the covenant does not feel imposed upon them. However, in the spirit of collaboration and connection, you'll find a sample leadership covenant below and in the resource section. Here is an example of a simple board covenant, titled "The Rules of the Road," which can be adapted for your context:

The Rules of the Road
A Leadership Board Covenant for the Small Church

Decisions are Made by the Board Members Who Show Up:

- The charge conference elects the Leadership Board and Committee on Nominations and Leadership Development in accordance with the *Book of Discipline of the United Methodist Church.*

- Except for official trustee legal business (which has a majority attendance requirement for a quorum), the *Discipline* defines a quorum as those members of a committee who are present.

- Leadership Board members are expected to attend all board meetings unless ill or out of town. If needed, members can be tied into meetings via speaker phones or video chat. If members miss more than three meetings per year, the board chair will converse with the board member to see if their seat needs to be vacated and filled by someone who can be more active.

- Teleconference or online meeting participation is okay if allowed by the group, but the United Methodist Church does not authorize voting "proxies."

- The board will move into a confidential "executive session" whenever Pastor-Parish Relations Committee work is being done. Only official PPRC members can be present for that component of the meeting, and all the appropriate PPRC restrictions of the *Book of Discipline* apply.

- Leadership Board members will review the meeting packet prior to meetings and come fully prepared and ready to participate.

- During a duly called and advertised meeting, we don't delay board business because someone is missing unless there are extenuating circumstances, such as foul weather.

Leadership Board Members are Disciples of Jesus and Fiduciary Officers:

- Board members carry, support, and promote the mission and vision of the church at all times.

- Leadership Board members are role models for the congregation. Therefore, members will model mature discipleship by being present in worship at least three times per month, giving proportionally, having an active prayer life, serving in mission three times per year, being active on a ministry team, being in a consistent faith development group, and openly share their faith with others in the secular world.

- Leadership Board members will encourage and support their pastor and fellow board members.

- Leadership Board members will hold ourselves, the pastor, and other board members accountable for their leadership roles and responsibilities. This includes allowing others to hold the board members collectively and individually accountable.

- Leadership Board members shall recuse themselves from any situation that could be construed as a conflict of interest.

- Leadership Board members have no special or unique personal authority or ability to demand time or actions from the pastor or staff outside that work assigned by the Leadership Board.

- Leadership Board members will act in good faith, serving out of loyalty to the mission of the church, obedience to the *Book of Discipline of the United Methodist Church,* and policies set forth by the charge conference and annual conference, and faithfulness to their duties as board members.

Leadership Board members hold one another in daily prayer.

We Will Speak the Truth in Love (Ephesians 4:15)

- Communication will be respectful, open, and honest. As a Leadership Board, we will approach matters of disagreement with transparency and maintain our missional focus on making disciples of Jesus Christ. Board members will not participate in "parking lot conversations" related to their role as a board member.

- Leadership Board members understand that conflict and disagreements are natural in any community, including the church. When approached by a person or group concerning a matter of disagreement or conflict, we will follow the path laid out by Jesus in Matthew 18 by encouraging the concerned party to go directly to the individual or by volunteering to go with the concerned party as an supportive presence. In accordance with the *Discipline of the United Methodist Church,* the pastor will be present in all meetings unless the pastor is voluntarily absent. At no time will we support or participate in secret meetings that undermine the integrity or authority of the pastor or the Leadership Board.

- Leadership Board members are representatives of the Leadership Board at all times during their leadership terms. Leadership Board members have a fiduciary duty to the Leadership Board and the church to uphold the highest standards of integrity in relationships and to support the mission of the congregation, including publicly supporting other congregational leaders, staff, ministry leaders, and clergy of the congregation.

- Leadership Board members will hold each other accountable as disciples of Jesus and as church leaders through our prayers, presence, gifts, service, and witness.

The Leadership Board (in its role of PPRC) will hold the pastor accountable in collaboration with the bishop and district superintendent.

We Will Balance Transparency and Confidentiality

- The United Methodist Church supports open meetings (BOD ¶ 722) at all levels of the church. Exceptions are Pastor-Parish Relations Committee work and some legal work of the Trustees, such as property negotiations.

- The Leadership Board, in its role and responsibility as the Pastor-Parish Relations Committee, is held to a high standard of confidentiality in personnel and clergy appointment matters.

- Board members understand that as leaders, derogatory comments or conversations about personnel (especially the pastor) are inappropriate and to be avoided. Concerns will be processed with the collective Leadership Board and the district superintendent only.

- The Leadership Board will move into executive session for some agenda items, particularly the work as the Pastor-Parish Relations Committee. In those cases, a separate set of minutes for the session shall be kept, and those not on the board should be excused from the meeting.

No secret meetings are allowed, and when the Leadership Board is doing the business of the Pastor-Parish Relations Committee, the pastor shall be present (see BOD ¶ 258.2 for particulars).

We Are a Leadership Board with a Unified Voice

- Leadership Board members are encouraged to invest in board conversations and decisions with vigor and passion. However, once the board has come to a decision, each Leadership Board member will openly and publicly support the decision of the Leadership Board whether the individual member personally agrees with the decision. A unified voice and message from the Leadership Board are essential.

- Board members will not call out or undermine the collective decisions of the board.

Because small churches are highly relational and often involve people who are related, a "State of Grace" document may be a suitable substitute for a leadership covenant. This alternative does not eliminate or lessen accountability for leadership but focuses on the high value of relationship as the primary driver. Of course, the example will need to be adapted, but it is a good starting place.

A Leadership Board may want to combine the relational qualities of the "State of Grace" document with the accountability elements in the sample "Rules of the Road" leadership covenant. For more information, visit:

co-intelligence.org/P-StateOfGraceDocument.html

Leadership Board's Work Summary

The work of the Leadership Board in the simplified, accountable structure may likely be quite different if you are new to the model of simplified structure and/or accountable leadership. But let us assure you that once you have transitioned fully into the model, your work as a Leadership Board will be much more effective, efficient, and focused. You'll be able to accomplish more, be more missionally focused, and simultaneously be more permission-giving to the ministry teams. Living into this new model takes a culture shift, but it is certainly worth the effort.

Team Questions

1. Compare the suggested agenda to your current agenda. What shifts need to be made to adopt the suggested agenda? How open is your leadership to making these shifts? What kind of impact might these shifts have on the work of the Leadership Board?

2. Does your church currently have a set of guiding principles? If so, what additional guiding principles might your Leadership Board consider that would offer even more permission to ministry coordinators and your pastor? If your church does not have guiding principles, how would the development of such make the ministries of your church more effective and easier for those who lead them?

3. Does your current Leadership Board have a leadership covenant? If so, what might you want to add? How well are your leaders holding one another accountable to the covenant? If your board does not have a leadership covenant, when might your leaders consider adopting one? How might adopting a leadership covenant help leaders live into an accountable leadership model?

CHAPTER EIGHT

Simplifying Structure in Multiple Church Charges & Cooperative Parishes

In the United Methodist Church, smaller congregations are often linked together as a multi-point charge/circuit or a cooperative parish. In cases where a congregation is considering moving toward a simplified, accountable leadership structure but the church is linked with a congregation that follows a more traditional structure, be sure to include the district superintendent in the conversation about the conference's expectations for sharing the work of the Pastor-Parish Relations Committee (PPRC). If multiple churches are considered to be a single charge (one appointment), it is appropriate to have a single PPRC consisting of members from each church to represent the interests and ministry of all congregations. One solution is for the Nominating Committee to assign a few members from your Leadership Board to be representatives on the combined charge PPRC (including the lay leaders and the charge's lay member of annual conference) and to have those assignments approved as part of your church/charge conference.

In cooperative parishes, wide latitude is provided for structuring the relationship between multiple congregations. Your Leadership Board may serve as the congregation's PPRC and relate to the other PPRCs in the parish, or a separate charge PPRC may need to be created by your charge conference. Your district superintendent will certainly have some expectations around these options. Additionally, in some flavors of cooperative parish, there are options to create a single parish or charge council to oversee the ministries of all the worshiping and ministry locations.

In all these options, a multi-point charge or cooperative parish will want to ensure representation from all the congregations. For instance, if three congregations of similar size are on a charge together in a cooperative parish model, then the Parish Leadership Board of nine people would be made up of three people from each congregation (preferably one from each class).

The diagram below outlines a possible governance structure of a cooperative parish. You will note that each congregation has a local Board of Trustees and Nominations. The Board of Trustees can be small, with a minimum of three people in successive classes. When each church is a separate legal entity—separate 501(c)(3) nonprofit status and separate employer identification number—each church will need a separate Board of Trustees to handle legal concerns and property issues.

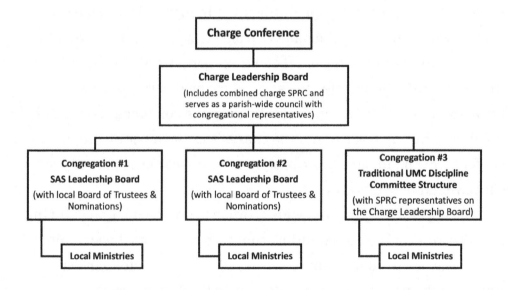

A Multi-Point Charge or Cooperative Parish utilizing the SAS Model

- The Charge Leadership Board/Cooperative Parish Council works with local church boards to adopt guiding principles for the Charge Leadership Board's operations. These guiding principles should outline the purpose of the Charge Leadership Board, demarcate shared work versus local church responsibilities, define the cooperative's ministry focus or purpose, and designate the limits of authority and responsibility of the Charge Leadership Board.

- The Charge Leadership Board coordinates with the congregations to rotate the charge conference election of lay members of the annual conference.

- Local churches retain the responsibility and authority of the Boards of Trustees (as part of the SAS Leadership Board) because of legal responsibilities and liabilities, including insurance and child protection policies.

- Local churches continue to have independent Nominations Committees that select the congregation's Leadership Board and appoint representatives to the charge Leadership Board.

- Staff, supervised by the pastor, may be amenable to the local church SAS or the charge board, depending on the nature of the staff position. For instance, some churches support a single charge administrative assistant as part of a charge. Job descriptions, organizational charts, and guiding principles must be clear to which governing body the staff are accountable to.

- Local church simplified, accountable structures
  and traditional structures may exist side by side in
  congregations yoked together as a cooperative. If one of
  the local churches on the charge is not ready to transition
  to the SAS model, the congregation can keep its legacy
  committee structure and appoint representatives to the
  charge Leadership Board.

CHAPTER NINE

How to Get There:
The Phases of Simplified, Accountable Structure (SAS)

If your church uses the traditional church structure consisting of the four administrative committees (Trustees, Finance, Staff-Parish Relations, and Church Council), you may be wondering about the process of moving to the simplified, accountable structure (SAS). In this chapter, we will provide an overview of the three phases of moving into SAS. For the comprehensive process, refer to *Mission Possible 3+*. This resource will cover the nuances of transitioning for small churches. The three phases for transitioning from the traditional structure to the simplified, accountable structure are Discerning, Equipping, and Implementing.

When we first started working with churches moving to this structure more than a dozen years ago, no resources or best practices were yet developed. Church leaders simply jumped into the deep end and did their best to figure it out. Along the way, we have identified what works and what doesn't and even shifted some best practices along the way.

One important lesson we have learned in this journey is not to rush the transition process and to proceed with the utmost transparency. This transparency helps build trust in the new structure from the onset. Too often, church leaders are under the false impression that moving to SAS is just a few simple technical changes: having fewer meetings and requiring the election of fewer leaders. With this mindset, the change is made quickly and oftentimes in charge conferences with only a handful of leaders. The result is often a congregation that feels run over by a small group of seemingly "secret," hand-picked leaders, and nobody knows what they are doing. The simplified, accountable structure model may be just what the congregation needs, but it doesn't have a chance to succeed because of the way it was rolled out. It is for this main reason—and a few others—that the three phases were developed. Following the steps in the three phases assures congregational leaders of the healthiest transitional process possible.

The Discerning Phase

The Discerning Phase is the first step in considering the adoption and implementation of the simplified, accountable structure. We have found discernment to be foundational in the process. This phase includes starting the conversation in the local church to explore the SAS model; requesting permission from the district superintendent to explore a simplified, accountable structure; communicating with the local congregation and providing information to them regarding the model; and ultimately, discernment of the congregation and its leaders to determine if this is the right model in the right season for the church.

Who is involved in this phase?

The phase is initially led by the council chair, lay leader, and pastor, with a SAS Discernment Team and SAS Prayer Team added along the way. Your congregation's leadership will need to consult with your district superintendent, and some conferences may have SAS-certified coaches (highly recommended) to journey with you in your process.

What is the timing of this phase?

Ideally, this phase is started in the first quarter of the calendar year if the church intends to move to the model the following January 1st. This phase should not be rushed and will be approximately three to six months. If there is a well-developed conference culture of SAS and the congregation is smaller, it will take much less time than in situations in which SAS seems like a brand new concept and there are several leaders.

On the next page is a very brief overview of the steps in the Discerning Phase. Note that there is work for the Church Council before step one of the Discerning Phase begins to arrive at the missional "why" you wish to consider moving to the simplified, accountable structure. These steps are covered in detail in the third edition of *Mission Possible: A Simple Structure for Missional Effectiveness*.

Steps in the SAS Discerning Phase

1. Church Council votes to explore SAS after assessing the missional "why" for considering the model

2. Letter from Council Chair and Pastor to DS seeking permission to explore the SAS model.

3. Approval received from DS to explore the SAS model and assignment of a SAS coach.

4. The SAS coach works with Council Chair and Pastor to establish a SAS Prayer Team and SAS Discernment Team to lead in learning, organizing, and communicating the SAS discernment process.

5. The SAS Discernment Team implements the communication and information plan with the congregation documenting congregational feedback.

6. Based on congregational feedback and leadership discernment, the Church Council submits a letter to DS to request approval to move to (or not) a SAS model.

7. DS reaches out to the SAS coach for feedback and makes a decision.

8. DS approves the church's move to SAS via letter, including the church conference date/time.

9. SAS coach begins to work with the Committee on Nominations and continues to work with church leaders on communication strategies (see Equipping Phase).

10. Church conference to approve SAS model.

11. The Nominations Committee completes its work.

12. Church/charge conference to approve new nominated leaders for the new SAS structure.

Note: After completing the Discerning Phase, move into Phase Two: Equipping, and then onto Phase Three: Implementing. We highly recommend partnering with a SAS-certified coach through all three phases for the most effective and healthiest transition and outcome!

The Equipping Phase

The Equipping Phase is the second step following the Discerning Phase. This phase involves training the Committee on Nominations and Lay Leadership Development members and the new Leadership Board members to prepare and support them in their leadership roles in the simplified, accountable leadership.

Who is involved in this phase?

The certified SAS coach first equips the Nominations Committee in its work for the adaptive approach in discerning the new leaders for the Leadership Board. Once the Leadership Board is elected, the coach will work with the members to equip them for their new role.

What is the timing of this phase?

This Equipping Phase begins as soon as the church conference adopts the simplified, accountable leadership structure. Ideally, this is midyear when the Nominations Committee's equipping begins. The Leadership Board's equipping is generally in November or early December so the members will be equipped when officially seated in their new position on January 1.

A Word of Encouragement and Caution

Remember, a third of the members roll off the Leadership Board and the Nominations Committee annually, so ongoing, annual equipping is crucial! SAS is a whole new method of leading churches. It is a large cultural shift, and it will therefore take years for this to become the natural leadership style default. Without ongoing SAS leadership training for both the Committee on Nominations and the Leadership Board, in three years, all new people will likely be serving without training on the new SAS structure and leadership model. Their default will be to go back to the only way of leading the church they know. The simplified structure will remain, but the traditional leadership practices will creep back into place. This is not a recommended leadership style nor a safe and effective leadership method. Therefore, we highly encourage having newly elected leaders trained each year to continue the leadership equipping and cultural shifts.

The Implementing Phase

The Implementing Phase is the third step in the process after the Equipping Phase. This phase is identified as the first year of the Leadership Board actually leading the church using the simplified, accountable structure. During this phase, the Leadership Board creates the initial guiding principles, their first leadership covenant, church policies and procedures (if not already completed), holds the first strategic ministry planning retreat, and begins living into both the technical and adaptive leadership changes in this model. The Leadership Board also grows into leading with accountability. This includes the Nominations Committee, too, as they journey through their first season of selecting two to three new leaders for the Leadership Board that will be rolling off after the first year and creating an intentional leadership development plan.

Who is involved in this phase?

The Implementing Phase's primary players are the new Leadership Board members and the pastor. The Nominations Committee members are also involved but in a different capacity. The certified SAS coach continues to play a key role as a resourcer, supporter, and accountability partner.

What is the timing of this phase?

The Implementing Phase is the first year during which the new simplified, accountable structure is utilized in the local church. However, most churches discover that it often takes years to fully live into a leadership culture with these technical and adaptive changes while practicing accountable leadership. Additionally, new clergy may be appointed to the church without experience in this model. Clergy new to the model will need additional equipping, coaching, and guidance during their first year in this model.

Insights and Small Church Adaptations to the Three Phases

While much of the process and steps through the three phases remain the same for small churches, a few adaptations will be helpful to consider.

- For small churches, communication is typically quicker and easier. Therefore, the Discerning Phase tends to be closer to three months rather than six months.

- Many churches, regardless of size, are tempted to skip over the steps for the Church Council to discern "why" the church is considering the model and to perform a SWOT (strengths, weaknesses, opportunities, and threats) analysis for transitioning and implementing SAS. A small church is especially tempted to do so. We urge you not to skip these critical steps. The "why" conversation helps the Church

Council dig deeper than the initial technical reasons for considering the model, such as having fewer meetings and requiring fewer elected leaders. The "why" conversations force the Church Council into the missional and adaptive reasons for adopting the model.

- Furthermore, when the leaders of the Church Council think deeply and strategically through each step of the SWOT analysis, they identify information upfront that they might not otherwise consider or think about. For example, leaders might identify potential pitfalls that can help them decide it's not the right time to make the switch or identify barriers they will need to address with the congregation upfront. Or leaders might discover a strength of SAS they had not considered before and can now communicate this new insight with the congregation during the discernment process.

- The Discerning Phase is also a time for the Church Council to be sure they are having the right conversation. Too often, SAS conversations are substituted when other conversations are too difficult to conduct. For example, we are often asked what to do if there are not enough people in the congregation to fulfill the required slots for the Leadership Board and Nominations Committee. First, if a small congregation cannot fill the leadership requirements for SAS, they certainly aren't currently able to fill them for the traditional structure. Secondly, if the congregation does not have enough people to fill in the small number of leaders, are there even people left to do the ministry, the most important job in the church? Third, if the church is this small, is a formal nonprofit 501(c)(3) corporation with a facility and overhead expenses really needed? Is there a more appropriate right-sized organizing entity with more faithful stewardship accountability?

- In a small church, the Discernment Team may be the same

people currently serving on the Church Council. However, if possible, invite people not currently on the Church Council to serve on the Discernment Team.

- The Discernment Team's communication plan will likely be much simpler, with fewer steps than other larger churches' plans. Again, fewer gatherings will be required due to fewer people, and the need for other means of communication will be less since much of the communication is handled relationally and informally in the small church. However, do not completely skip this step. At least one informational gathering will still be needed to explain why SAS is being considered, what it is, how it will improve the life of the church, what changes will occur, what the steps are for implementation, and to give people an opportunity to ask questions.

- For a ready-made leadership development process or at least a resource to help your Committee on Nominations and Leadership Development get started initially, check out *Launching Leaders: Taking Leadership Development to New Heights.*[23]

- On-demand SAS equipping for nominations, Leadership Boards, and the United Methodist Church *Book of Discipline,* "My Job" (disciplinary responsibilities and authority) is available if your church does not have access to a certified SAS coach:

kaykotan.com/sas-2/

Again, this overview is not meant to substitute for the comprehensive process outlined for the three phases in *Mission Possible 3+.* This overview is offered here as a glance to gain an overall understanding of the complete transition process. In addition,

---

[23] Kay Kotan and Phil Schroeder, *Launching Leaders: Taking Leadership Development to New Heights* (Market Square Books, August 2019).

we feel it is important to offer some nuances we have discovered in working with small churches in these three phases of transition. We can't stress enough how important it is to follow the process. While it does take a bit longer and a few extra steps, the church enters SAS in a much healthier place, more aware of the pathway ahead, and leaders are more fully equipped and prepared to lead in the new model.

SECTION

3

Simplified Approaches to Leading to Ministry

CHAPTER TEN
Simple Ministry Planning

Why plan ministries? Can't we all just show up? Well. . . we suppose that's possible, but it is certainly not the best stewardship of everyone's time and valuable ministry funds. The small church often operates on a thin margin of sustainability and accountability to the mission Jesus Christ has given us. The church is called to be stewards of Jesus' people and resources, all for the building up of the Kingdom of God. We believe those are reasons enough to invest in some simple planning!

As you consider the different expressions of ministry in this section, take note of some common principles for simple ministry planning in the small church. First, you will find the quick list of principles followed by a more detailed dive into each principle:

- **We, Not They** – "All Hands on Deck" is the rule, not the exception, so plan with all active attendees of all ages being involved in implementing the ministry, and include the assets of the larger community.

- **Get Face-to-Face** – Focus on building relationships, not complex systems.

- **Evangelism is not an Extra** – Embed evangelism (reaching new people for Jesus) into every ministry, every event, and every opportunity.

- **Dream Up a Team Up** – Partner with local institutions and nonprofits, especially for organizing the infrastructure for community ministry, leaning on their expertise and organization.

- **Deep, Not Wide** – Who is God calling you to build relationships with? Choose one niche and go deep relationally and with ministries for this one group. You'll reach more people using fewer resources without burning your volunteers out.

- **When in Doubt, Experiment** – Allow yourselves to try ministry experiments. In a season when many of our inherited ways of doing ministry are no longer effective, try something new every season or at least twice a year.

- **Simple with a Signature** – Instead of having multiple low-impact ministries, take a simple approach by discerning and focusing on one or two signature ministries.

- **Keep Accountable** – Be good stewards of God's people and resources by pruning ministries regularly and using the Accountable Leadership Cycle to keep the church on track and always learning.

We, Not They

The small church has a certain bandwidth of ministry opportunity and capacity. From potlucks to community VBS and weekly worship to soup kitchens, for many ministries to succeed, events and programs need to be "all hands on deck," with the entire congregation pitching in to help make ministry happen. Please realize that this is a gift. Large congregations often only have a fraction of their active membership ever show up for anything, much less participate.

Once early in his ministry, Blake accompanied his small church on an "all church" mission trip to an out-of-state mission depot after some flooding in the Midwest. Actually, twenty members were on the weeklong trip, which is a pretty good percentage for a church that usually worshiped around a hundred then. There were a half-dozen teens (with the very part-time youth director), a couple of older elementary children (and designated adults to serve as their guardians), and some adults of all generations, including one who used a walker. The whole church raised funds for the trip. A nurse, who was also a reserve military officer, organized the whole endeavor. Two of the youth weren't members, but a church member stepped up and made sure all the teens—especially the nonmembers—could attend at no cost. Those two youth were baptized and offered their testimony when the group returned. Only the small church could have imagined an experience such as this, and every member of the church could feel the presence of Jesus Christ in the endeavor because everyone, young and old, was involved in this intergenerational mission trip.

"We, not They" is also about recognizing the assets of the community itself. Your community is not just a place to donate time, talent and treasure; the community has assets as well. There are people in the community who are able to use *their* gifts, not just receive *our* gifts. So, celebrate and utilize the assets of the community, and include community members in your planning and ministry. God's wants to see the bigger "WE" at work.

Get Face-to-Face

Relationships are the heart of ministry. When Blake served as the executive pastor of a large metropolitan church, he had to manage ministry by the numbers: staffing, crowds, hospitality systems, discipleship pathways, room assignments, and schedule negotiations. These systems had to be continually maintained and nurtured.

Complex, intentional systems are necessary when a large church seeks to be fruitful and effective. Systems thrive on predictability, but in the small church, a single change in membership—deaths, moves, illness, or a new member—can radically change a church's future plans, and so systems usually create anxiety instead of building trust.

The gift of small churches, however, is intimacy—doing life together as disciples of Jesus. So, lean into this giftedness by always placing relationships first, beginning with every member's relationship with Jesus Christ and then relationships with other congregants, participants, and the community. There is a reason that bed & breakfast accommodations thrive even amid huge hotel chains: some folks are looking for intimacy, not anonymity. While the big church may have a small group for every generation and a classroom for every child's grade level, the small church can nurture an intergenerational community. Plan ministries that encourage this sort of intimacy and community as a reflection of God's very Triune nature.

Evangelism is not an Extra

You will not find a separate chapter on evangelism (making new disciples) in this book, but it's not because evangelism is unimportant. On the contrary, evangelism is so important we recommend that every ministry plan have evangelism embedded in it. While this should be true of any size church, it is vital for small churches. If your church simply does not have the bandwidth for a separate ministry to reach new people, care should be taken to consider ways that every single ministry—food pantry, Bible studies, VBS, mission Saturdays to build wheelchair ramps, Christmas caroling, booths at community festivals—is an opportunity to meet neighbors, share God's love, and invite others into friendship. This will mean planning ahead to have an "empty chair" at Bible studies, and reminding every member that it is our common responsibility to fill it. It also means encouraging folks to bring a "plus one" to help on mission projects. Since relationships are front and center in small churches, it reminds us to always reach beyond our friends within the congregation and toward those in the community who need Christ. Relational evangelism is at the core of our ministry planning and should be natural.

Dream Up a Team Up

Both rural and neighborhood small churches can discover huge benefits from partnerships with local institutions, schools, and nonprofits. First, the local community itself is strengthened by building relationships inside and outside the congregation. Second, the church can share or even offload logistics to partners, allowing the congregation to focus on relational ministry. Third, the church can rely on expertise and access from partners. Finally, and most importantly, teaming up can often produce a larger Kingdom impact with more people reached for Christ. Blake wrote about small church partnerships in a 2021 article for *Ministry Matters:*

> *Instead of building a new homemade-from-scratch ministry for the nutritionally insecure in your community, connect with a nonprofit, county senior center, or neighboring church, and see how your whole congregation could show up to make a difference. Instead of building an in-house literacy ministry that will be hard to staff and resource with members and money, team up with the local school to provide tutoring. Partnerships leave all the systems, processes, and bureaucracy to the experts, while the disciples of your church can provide the people-power to make an impact.*[24]

As you search for low-hanging fruit, we suggest two options for your first team-ups: the local school and/or your neighboring church of the same denomination. Local schools offer a place to impact lives,

---

[24] Blake Bradford, "Leading the Small Church from The Porch Swing," Ministry Matters, October 17, 2021, https://www.ministrymatters.com/lead/entry/11074/leading-the-small-church-from-the-porch-swing.

and the school's principal, counselor, or social worker can help you identify needs. As for teaming up with another nearby church, your writers come from the United Methodist tradition and have been formed in the spirit of connectionalism. We have seen how shared ministries and cooperative parishes have been transformative. We will offer more information about this vision for ministry in Chapter 8.

Deep, Not Wide

Not even the largest church can "connect with everybody." Certainly, anyone God brings to your doorstep should be welcomed, included, and adopted into the church family. And the Holy Spirit is great at surprising us by bringing us people we didn't expect. But that being said, your church leadership should be asking, "Who is God calling us to build relationships with?" Choose one niche population and go deep relationally and with ministries for this one group. You'll reach more people using fewer resources without burning your volunteers out.

In a consultation with one congregation, the leaders were adamant that they wanted to focus on families with young children. No other option was to be considered. As the leaders started diving deep into the demographics provided by the conference office, they discovered that there were incredibly few young families in their community. Instead, their community was filled with baby boomers, many of whom had moved into the community in retirement. Upon further discernments— including studying demographics and also a focus group with some friends from a local civic group—the leaders decided to make a shift after they realized that many of the retirees who were moving to the area didn't have a church home and many didn't have a faith tradition. By "going deep" on boomer ministry, the church could reach an unchurched generation and offer them meaning for their lives, community, and a discipling relationship with Jesus.

When in Doubt, Experiment

Focusing on sustainability is not the same as battening down the hatches and staying stuck in our comfort zone. Allow yourselves to try ministry experiments. In a season when many of our inherited ways of doing ministry are no longer effective, try something new every season or at least twice a year. Use the Accountable Leadership Cycle to plan, set reasonable goals, evaluate the experiment, and just DO SOMETHING! Sometimes experiments fail; that's ok. A culture of ministry experimentation comes with the idea that some experiments simply don't work out as hoped or planned. At worst, you will learn something. At best, folks will discover and experience the love of Jesus Christ.

Simple with a Signature

Instead of having multiple low-impact ministries, take a simple approach by discerning and focusing on one or two signature ministries: perhaps one for equipping disciples and one for local community impact. These signature ministries may change with the seasons or have a cycle of a few years, but focusing on a few high-impact signature ministries will build momentum and community awareness. Check out *Expanding the Expedition Through Community Connection* by Dan Pezet.[25] It is a great resource for helping congregations understand the value of signature ministries and how to identify and adopt one.

If your church currently has several "private ministries" led by different members with personal passions, the Leadership Board can start having conversations with these members about combining resources. For instance, the diaper ministry and the food pantry might be combined by focusing both ministries on the same families with a holistic approach. Or if a "ministry" is really one person's

---

[25] Dan Pezet, *Expanding the Expedition Through Community Connection* (Market Square Publishing, December 2021).

passion, release them to serve on their own, but unhitch the church from this ministry to more fully concentrate on fewer ministries done with excellence and stronger relationship building.

Keep Accountable

In Chapter 3, we shared the importance of accountable leadership. We encourage your Leadership Board to practice and model the Accountable Leadership Cycle to encourage a culture of accountability to Christ's mission for the church. This cycle begins with the church's mission, research, and goal-setting and guides the board in following up with evaluation and reflection. Using this tool, especially for evaluation, will allow you to depersonalize the evaluation experience, focusing on the ministry instead of feelings of blame or failure:

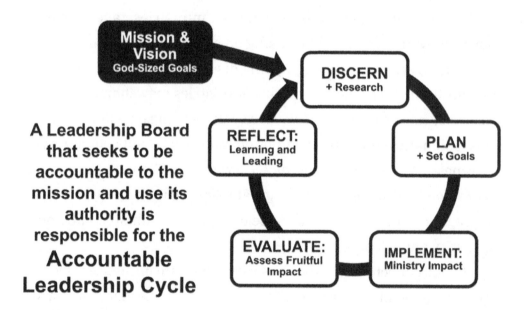

Accountable Leadership Cycle	
Mission, Vision, & Purpose (God-sized Goals)	Ministries should come out of your mission, vision, and goals. Accountability is ultimately rooted in following Christ's mission for the congregation.
Discern + Research	The first step of the cycle is to discern ministry needs as rooted in the mission. That takes prayerful conversation and research such as demographic studies, neighborhood prayer walks, conversations with the local school principal or mayor, and listening to neighbors.
Plan + Set Ministry **Goals**	The ministry team and coordinator should plan and set goals for the proposed ministry, including trackable measurements. For example, a "bridge event" to connect with neighbors will need plans for members to greet and get to know guests, not just "run the event." Similarly, a goal for such an event would be appropriate guest follow-up within twenty-four hours and meaningfully connecting with one new family. Ministries without planned goals for transformational impact become random "feel-good events." The ministry team should create clear goals as part of their ministry planning.
Implement: Ministry Impact	The responsible ministry team is now ready to execute the plan using the predefined goals. Ultimately, every serving disciple on the team (and the church) is accountable to the mission of the particular ministry and the congregation's larger overall mission and vision. Impactful ministries seek to make disciples and transform the world.
Evaluate: Assess Fruitful Impact	The ministry team should assess the ministry from proposal to event to follow-up and thank you notes. What worked well? What needed work? What surprised the team? What was the Kingdom impact? Using the goals for the ministry, how did the ministry measure up? What did the team learn? Were there any Holy Spirit sightings during the ministry? This evaluation is a vital step in accountability.
Reflect: Learning and Leading	A solid evaluation allows the coordinator and pastor to learn about the mission field and the congregation's capacity for ministry follow-through. This reflection time is different from an evaluation. While an evaluation is about doing things right, reflection is about doing the right things. Reflection is a skill and an intentional practice that invites the congregation's leaders back into the season of prayerful learning and discernment about the congregation's future.

Adapted from *Mission Possible 3+, page 124 and Strengthening Decision-Making and Governance,* page 72.

125

The reflection step is as helpful as it is rare. As stewards of the church's resources, the board is ultimately responsible for deciding which ministries need to be encouraged and which need to be paused or concluded. Since the 2020 COVID shutdowns, I (Blake) have used the metaphor of a kitchen to describe the sorting process church leaders need to use in order to assess their capacity to keep or let go of ministries.

If you start with what's cooking on the stove, you see four burners. The challenge is that small churches probably don't have four burners on their stoves, even on the best of days. That would require many more disciples and financial resources than the small church has access to, especially in a COVID-impacted season where resources are tighter and actively engaged people are fewer. These days, some of us are operating on a hotplate, not a stovetop! The ministries that belong on the stove are the ones that have been assessed as the most fruitful and effective and, upon reflection by the board, best fulfill the church's mission. Some ministries may go on the countertop for preparation and planning and perhaps for the right season when the "hot" ministries have concluded. Some ministries, or perhaps ministry ideas, are not ripe for today's season or require resources beyond the church's capacity. These great ideas must be put in the refrigerator—or perhaps the freezer. And some ministries, although beloved—I'm looking at you, 27th Annual Pumpkin Patch!— need to go into the deep freezer in the garage with last year's deer meat or maybe even in the compost bin.

Part of accountable leadership is knowing when to compost or deep freeze ministries. Let go of some ministries that are no longer effective. These ministries that are no longer effective may have been designed for a different context or era or to solve a problem that no longer exists. It may be that the people who were passionate about it have moved on or even passed on to the Church Triumphant.

The ministry may be less effective now because it simply wore out its welcome. In any case, the Leadership Board needs to practice accountability and make the hard call. Celebrate the life and fruitfulness of the ministry, but give it a funeral and let it rest in peace.

Returning our attention to the stovetop burners, accountable leadership is not only about what to put in the deep freeze, but it is much more about how to really pay attention to what's cooking on the stove—your ongoing and signature ministries. By focusing (deep, not wide) and staying within the church's capacity, folks tend to stay excited, energized, and on mission. The church is more sustainable, and your ministries are more impactful.

Team Questions

1. Take inventory of the common principles for simple ministry planning for small churches. Which principles are your church following? Which ones are not being followed?

2. Looking over the principles list again, which principle or two, if adopted, would have the most profound positive impact on the life of the church?

3. Identify the steps for implementing the identified principles to adopt. Once those principles are adopted, choose another one. Repeat the process until all principles have been adopted, implemented, and working effectively.

CHAPTER ELEVEN

Simplifying Ministry for the Small Church

Mission & Evangelism through Partnerships

Most of us have heard the old saying Allen F. Morgenstern made famous back in the 1930s, "Work smarter, not harder." Your community is filled with wonderful people with gifts and assets for ministry. Rather than starting from scratch or implementing every ministry individually by church, look for opportunities to partner with great things already going on in the community that align with the mission of the church. For example, rather than locating and purchasing a lot, finding blueprints, providing all the financial resources, and recruiting all the volunteers to build a house for a family in need, simply partner with Habitat for Humanity. They are a well-known organization with a great national reputation. They know and can handle the logistics of house-building. A church can simply pick a day to bring a work crew, show up, and all the supplies and people needed to provide direction and expertise are already in place. Their mission certainly aligns with the church: "Seeking to put God's love into action, Habitat for Humanity brings people together to build homes, communities and hope."[26]

Not only is this a great service project for the congregation to get

---

[26] http://www.habitat.org/about/mission-and-vision.

involved in for their local community, but this is a great opportunity to invite a friend with a hammer to join you. In a culture that is no longer naturally drawn to the church (and sometimes even church adverse), inviting someone to help with a community project is a better strategy than inviting them to worship on Sunday in the church building. Younger generations are more eager to serve than show up on a Sunday morning. In addition, there will likely be more opportunities for meaningful conversation while serving together than in a worship experience anyway.

> Mission Projects
>
> can also serve as
>
> evangelism opportunities
>
> with taglines such as
>
> "Bring a Friend with a Hammer."

Another great example of this type of ministry in action is The Forge in Vancouver, Washington. Matt Overton has a passion for youth ministries, but he knew the traditional youth ministries model (gathering at the church on Sunday night for food, study, and activity) was just not as effective as it once was. He felt there had to be a better way to connect with youth. He realized that whenever the kids gathered for a service project, more kids showed up, and more meaningful conversation and discipleship occurred than anything he had ever planned during those Sunday night gatherings. Over time, The Forge has morphed and expanded, but basically, it is a nonprofit organization that provides students with real-world work experience and project-based learning through community partners and mentors. Imagine a congregant who couldn't imagine how they could be helpful on those Sunday night gatherings being suddenly inspired to share their experience as a carpenter or a jewelry designer with youth eager to learn.[27]

Another way to partner with an existing event is to add a relational spin to something you might already be doing. I (Kay) was working with a church that participated in the city's annual festival by renting a booth space. In past years, they had given out water bottles or some other giveaway with the church's name on it. When asked what the purpose was for their participation in the event, they answered "outreach." (By the way, I have a confession. I've grown weary of the word *outreach.* I believe we have become scared of the word *evangelism,* so we decided outreach was a "nicer" way to talk about it. Unfortunately, what this has done is confused the meaning between mission [service] and evangelism [sharing the Good News of Jesus], as so many churches now refer to both of them collectively as "outreach.") When asked what they meant by "outreach," they eventually explained that they expected the recipient of the water bottle to show up on Sunday morning. How was that working for them? It was not!

I asked if they would be willing to try something different at the next festival. They agreed, but what? I asked who attended the festival and what product or service might be missing or helpful for them at the festival. After much head-scratching, they identified a gap and devised a great solution to close it. Families attended the festival, but there was nowhere for parents to change babies' diapers or mothers to nurse their babies. The church would host a free baby changing and nursing station. This approach would provide much more opportunity for conversation and relationship-building opportunities than a walk-

---

[27] To learn more about The Forge in Vancouver, Washington, visit https://thecolumbiafutureforge.com.

by water-bottle handoff. They even went a step further and offered a drawing for a gift certificate to a local children's specialty shop. They collected names and had a follow-up strategy to reach out to parents after the festival. Their booth was unique, much appreciated, and a huge success! Those serving at the booth made new friends and laid the foundation for new relationships.

Shared Ministry in Multi-Point Charges, Cooperative Parishes, and Multi-site Churches

Does this sound familiar? One small church struggles to provide a fruitful mission project, a vital children's ministry, and a men's group that provides meaningful relationships. The other two small churches in the charge struggle with the same challenges. Only a few miles separate these churches, yet each church is trying to create and sustain a full ministry offering all by itself. When resources are spread too thin, not only are volunteers being burned out, but too often, the church cannot offer its best, and therefore, the ministry is not fruitful.

Not one of these people, even though their lives of faith were exemplary,
got their hands on what was promised.
God had a better plan for us: that their faith
and our faith would come together to make one complete whole,
their lives of faith not complete apart from ours.

Hebrews 11:39-40 (MSG)

While the number of programs and activities may look good on the end-of-the-year statistics report, the church does not always take into consideration the resources expended (time, energy, dollars, people's limited capacity) in comparison to the ROI (return on investment: leveraging the blessings God has provided to disciple those already gathered and reach new people). The congregation has missions and programs without enough people to participate in them, and there is always a constant cry for volunteers. When two or more churches come together in cooperation, these challenges only increase because they are likely competing ministries or competing with shared resources.

However, when there is a shared vision for shared ministries within cooperative parishes or multi-point charges, there is a holistic approach rather than a competitive approach limited by the resources of one church. The leaders look at the collective mission field and the collective resources and then determine the unique needs of the mission field and the resources of each congregation to determine the signature ministry each congregation is best equipped and gifted to offer. Rather than duplicating ministries, each congregation offers one unique ministry they feel especially passionate about, resourced, and gifted to extend that meets a need in the shared mission field of the cooperative parish or multi-point charge.

Here is an example of how a multi-hub approach might work: One church in the charge becomes the hub for children's ministry where all children from the cooperative parish and the community gather for children's choir, special programs, and monthly or bi-monthly Sunday afternoon activities. Another church in the charge becomes the technology hub where all the websites are maintained, online worship is offered for all the churches in the charge, all social media is handled for all the churches, and the digital newsletter for the multi-point charge is created and distributed. The third congregation becomes the hub for all mission work. This might be a countywide food pantry and clothing closet where all the congregants from the cooperating congregations serve. Or perhaps it is the center where various work crews are dispatched to perform various community projects such as building wheelchair ramps, storm cleanup, minor home repairs for the elderly, yard cleanups, picking up trash along highways, or city park spring cleanup.

Here is an another example of different hub approach. Rather than a multi-hub, this example is a single hub. Typically, this model is the best approach in an extended ministry cooperative parish model when a larger church shares ministry with a smaller church(es). The larger church becomes the hub due to its expanded resources, staff, and centralized operations such as accounting, communications, and technology.

In the United Methodist Church *Book of Discipline,* ¶ 206 outlines ten different types of cooperative parishes. Within those ten, there is further opportunity for flexibility and creativity in how cooperative parishes are formed, how they function, and how they are staffed. There are two important factors to remember when considering a cooperative parish. First, cooperative parishes should not be a solution to an appointment problem. That is not a missional motivation. Instead, it is a survival motivation. To be a healthy model, a cooperative parish needs to be motivated by a shared vision of how God calls them to do ministry together. Second, it is by far a much healthier approach when it comes from the congregations rather than a judicatory leader.

When multiple churches share a discerned grassroots vision, the congregants are committed to the direction and own the decision. When a judicatory leader makes the decision for churches to come together as a cooperative parish, the congregations often feel imposed upon. There is no local church commitment or shared vision, so oftentimes, the cooperative parish fails. At best, it is a multi-charge appointment sharing a clergy salary package. If your church is interested in exploring a cooperative parish model, check out this resource, *An Effective Approach to Cooperative Parishes: A Congregational Guide to Discernment and Implementation* by Kay Kotan and Jason Stanley with the foreword by Blake Bradford.[28]

---

[28] Kay Kotan and Jason Stanley, *An Effective Approach to Cooperative Parishes: A Congregational Guide to Discernment and Implementation* (Market Square Publishing, August 2022).

The possibilities are truly endless. Just make sure the chosen model is based on the leaders' passions, the gifts of the congregations, the resources of the given location, and the needs of the community the cooperative parish serves.

Relational Ministries

It is always helpful to move beyond ministries being programs or events and shift our understanding that ministries are, first and foremost, relational. Ministries are how the church helps existing disciples grow deeper in their faith and how new people encounter Christ for the first time and take the first steps in their faith journey. Too often, we treat ministries as tasks rather than methods to grow relationships. All ministries are meant to be rooted in relationship:

- Grow in our relationship with Christ

- Grow in our Christlikeness

- Meet new people in the mission field God is calling us to reach

- Build deeper relationships with unchurched people in our mission field

- Share the Good News with new friends we have built relationships with in the community

- Encourage and hold others in our congregation accountable to grow in their faith

- Care for those in the community and congregation who are hurting or need help

We often conduct our ministries as transactions, with the church having all the assets and the community being those in need. This is especially true for mission projects. Transactional ministries are missional gestures: the church collects socks for the local school upon the school counselor's recommendation; it annually

135

collects health kits and school supplies and raises money for the local Habitat for Humanity. Let us be clear. There is nothing wrong with missional gestures. They meet a need. They are good things to do and a part of our discipleship journey to help others. We seem to think the missional gesture is the endpoint. Instead, think of missional gestures as the doorway to meet people where they are, to come alongside them, build a relationship, invest in their lives, and eventually, we might be able to share our faith story. If the church is to make disciples, the church needs to turn missional gestures into relationship-building opportunities. The best place to invest in these relationships is with the schools and established organizations like the local Habitat for Humanity.

When the shift is made from transactional to relational, the church will dig deeper to discover the relational need rather than only unearthing the outer layer need. For example, a church leader would discover this relational need through a more intentional conversation with the school counselor. Through that conversation, the church leader discovered the root cause of the need for those socks for the students when she heard the counselor sharing that families in the community need help planning a family budget. The church leader walked out with a two-part plan. First, the church will collect the socks to meet the immediate need. But second, and more importantly, the church will offer free finance and budget-planning classes for parents. These classes will provide the opportunity for building relationships with the parents and help solve the root cause of the sock issue (symptom). She even thought the cooperative parish could offer free childcare during the classes to invest in the families holistically. As a next step, the cooperative parish would offer a graduation party for the parents completing the budget-planning classes.

This is also an example of going deep rather than wide with ministries. Rather than collecting socks for the elementary school, hats for the housing challenged, canned goods for the local food pantry, school supplies for the junior high school, blankets for the women's shelter, and coats for the orphanage (all wonderful missional gestures), the church or cooperative parish could take the missional gesture of socks and take the first step through the relationship door with the family benefitting from the socks. That first step leads to a financial class, then to mentoring, a graduation celebration, and then to parents sharing their stories with other parents about becoming teachers at your next round of financial classes. As you begin to think relationally about ministry, you will discover new opportunities and ways to minister in and (more importantly) with the community. Some traditional ministries that took excessive time, energy, and people but had a low Kingdom impact can now be re-evaluated for relationship-building opportunities.

Along the way, don't imagine that the church has all the gifts and that the wider community is only a list of needs. Instead, every member of the community (both inside and outside the church) has assets, strengths, and gifts, and the church can be a place for everyone to live out God's giftedness.

Relational Discipleship

Some parents intentionally move into a community so their children can attend a particular school. Or they seek out schools that match the type of educational experience they want their children to have. In fact, some parents pay for a small-school experience when a public school experience would cost them nothing. Do you know why parents intentionally seek out small schools for their children to attend? The top benefits for small schools include the following:

- A strong sense of connection and high emphasis on relationships

- Ability to have more unique, individualized learning experiences

- Closer relationships with teachers and students of other ages

- A strong relationship with parents and staff—a sense of community or extended family

- Teachers report a higher level of job satisfaction and are therefore happier in their day-to-day interactions with the students, and there is less turnover. Consistent care from teachers who love what they are doing (obviously, it's not for the pay) makes for a happy environment for the children.

Take another look at the list above. Do you notice any parallels between some of the benefits of attending a small school and a small church? After translating from the school to the church context, which do you think are benefits for your church? Which do you believe could benefit from becoming involved in your small church?

Someone who chooses to attend a small church does not expect a large children's Sunday school class for every grade. If that's the kind of ministry they desired, they would be in a different church. People who have an affinity for small churches place a high value on close relationships. Larger churches may be able to offer more programs, but they struggle to provide those closer relationships that small churches are able to offer. Shine and take advantage of the strengths the small church offers. Let go of those impractical expectations that don't align with the small church. Sunday school or discipleship will likely be very intergenerational. Embrace it and get creative instead of fighting it, or you will end up having 1:1 teacher-to-student ratios. This is not a good use of resources! Dust off and reimagine a one-room Sunday school model. Use out-of-the-box ideas that will make multigenerational learning fun. Just to give you some ideas, check out these resources:

- dibletheology.com/bake-with-the-bible

- messychurchusa.org/messy-pathways/

- www.cokesbury.com/multi-age-quarterly-curriculum-comparison-chart

Relational Worship

Worship is an experience of all the senses. Different people experience Christ in worship in a variety of ways. Worship with impact provides opportunities for a variety of people to experience Christ. Some experience Christ in prayer, others with music or from the message, prayer, scripture, liturgy, video, printed material, or a take-home object. It is impossible for one clergyperson to continuously create an impactful worship experience solo. Solo-planned worship becomes stale and predictable.

Liturgy actually means the work of the people. Worship is an expression of the community's relationship with God, not a paint-by-number exercise by the pastor. A solo pastor, especially in the first year of ministry in a setting, often plans worship for a community that s/he does not completely know or understand.

I (Blake) vividly recall my first Easter morning as the "new pastor" at a church. I had served that congregation for months, and I thought I had asked all the right questions. I was doing the final set-up when one of the choir members arrived early to prepare. She asked me, "Where is the living cross?" "Huh?" "The living cross! Every Easter, we all bring flowers from our yards and gardens to place them in this wooden cross with chicken wire on it." So to the storage room we went until, sure enough, we found a large wooden box in the shape of a cross with chicken wire on the front of it. We managed to get it in place just before the crowd walked into the sanctuary. We never published anything about bringing flowers in any of the previous weeks' bulletins or newsletters, but almost everyone brought their flowers to place in the cross during the prelude.

The laity knew their traditions; it was their clergy—me—that was clueless. I could have preached the best sermon, and we could have sung all the favorite Easter hymns, but I know that the church would have eaten roasted preacher for Sunday dinner if I had neglected their beloved Easter tradition. By "taking care of business" in planning all the congregation's worship, I was leaving out the voices of the laity and setting myself up for failure. Lesson learned: worship leadership is meant to be shared between clergy AND laity.

Laity provides a plethora of spiritual gifts. Too often, those gifts are not utilized for the weekly worship experience. We often use our laity's musical talents (vocal and instrumental) but overlook other giftedness. Laity often bring other unique talents such as creativity, aesthetics and decor, resourcing video and graphics, thematic ideas, planning and organization, and topics for sermon consideration based on community needs, history, and experiences.

Not only are there opportunities for laity to help create the worship experience, but there are other opportunities to impact worship leadership, too. Gone are the days when the congregation desires to have the pastor lead the entire worship service as a master of ceremonies. Rather, people engage at a deeper level when multiple folks—including laity—lead worship. Opportunities for laity to lead worship include such things as responsive readings, serving as a worship leader or worship host, reading a poem or story, drama, dance, vocals, running sound and multimedia, instrumentalists, and more.

Here is a sampling of ideas to get your creative juices flowing:

- Have the children stay in the worship space for the entire service. Include them and their gifts whenever possible.

- The third grader can lead the offertory one week.

- The teen can do a trumpet or saxophone solo.

- Create a children's playground table at the front or back of the sanctuary that includes child-sized table and chairs, coloring sheets, and soft toys instead of sending them to the musty basement classroom.

- If there is only one youth, she may be your liturgist.

- Youth love technology. Televisions are cheap. Invite the youth to create digital images to reinforce the sermon's theme, words on the screen for the hymns, announcements to roll before service, free pre-service music to use as appropriate, etc.

- Invite youth or young adults to launch a simple online worship experience. Those that lead can invite their friends to help or join them. It's the best form of evangelism!

Congregational Care

No matter the size of the church, pastoral care needs to become congregational care. When we think of caring for the congregation's sick and homebound, the church often expects that this is the sole responsibility of the pastor. This is how the term "pastoral care" originated. Interestingly enough, John Wesley (founder of Methodism) never intended this, as he explains in his Sermon 98.[29]

First, Wesley addresses why we are called to care for the sick:

The walking herein is essentially necessary, as to the continuance of that faith whereby we are already saved grace, so to the attainment of everlasting salvation. Of this cannot doubt, if we seriously consider that these are the very words of the great Judge himself: "Come, ye blessed children of my Father, inherit the kingdom prepared for you from the foundation of the world.

For I was hungry, and ye gave me meat: Thirsty, and ye gave me drink: I was a stranger, and ye took me in: Naked, and ye clothed me: I was sick, and ye visited me: I was in prison, and ye came unto me." (Matt. 25:34, &c.)

"Verily, I say unto you, Inasmuch as ye have done it to the least of these my brethren, ye have done it unto me." If this does not convince you that the continuance in works of mercy is necessary to salvation, consider what the Judge of all says to those on the left hand. . . . "

---

[29] John Wesley, "On Visiting the Sick," Sermon 98 (text from the 1872 edition), *Christian Classics Ethereal Library,* http://www.wbbm.org/john-wesley-sermons/serm-098.htm.

In this passage, Wesley explains what is implied by visiting the sick:

> *By the sick, I do not mean only those that keep their bed, or that are sick in the strictest sense. Rather I would include all such as are in a state of affliction, whether of mind or body; and that whether they are good or bad, whether they fear God or not.*

Next, Wesley teaches that a doctor or a clergyperson can't fulfill a congregant's duty to visit. The doctor or clergy's visit does not eliminate a disciple's duty to also comfort the sick. It also doesn't help the one doing the act of mercy (me and you) grow in their discipleship unless it is face-to-face. As a disciple, if I don't visit the "sick" of all kinds, I lose the opportunity to experience the means of grace.

> *. . . you might have abundant opportunities of comforting those that are in pain of body, distress of mind; you might find opportunities of strengthening the feeble-minded, quickening those that are faint and weary; and of building up those that have believed, and encouraging them to "go on to perfection." But these things you must do in your own person; you see they cannot be done by proxy. Or suppose you could give the same relief to the sick by another, you could not reap the same advantage to yourself; you could not gain that increase in lowliness, in patience, in tenderness of spirit, in sympathy with the afflicted, which you might have gained, if you had assisted them in person. Neither would you receive the same recompense in the resurrection of the just, when "every man shall receive his own reward, according to his own labour."*

Finally, Wesley describes who is to visit the sick:

> *By whom is this duty to be performed? The answer is ready: By all that desire to "inherit the kingdom" of their Father, which was "prepared forth from the foundation of the world." For thus saith the Lord, "Come, ye blessed;—inherit the kingdom;—For I was sick, and ye visited me." And to those on the left hand, "Depart, ye cursed;—for I was sick, and ye visited me not." Does not this plainly imply, that as all who do this are "blessed," and shall "inherit the kingdom;" so all who do it not are "cursed," and shall "depart into everlasting fire?"*

Wesley closes with this summary:

> *Seeing then this is a duty to which we are called, rich and poor,*
> *young and old, male and female, let the time past suffice that almost*
> *all of us have neglected it, as by general consent. O what need has*
> *every one of us to say, "Lord, forgive me my sins of omission!" Well,*
> *in the name of God, let us now from this day set about it with general*
> *consent. And I pray, let it never go out of your mind that this is a*
> *duty which you cannot perform by proxy; unless in one only case,*
> *unless you are disabled by your own pain or weakness.*

Just like only learning the stories of Jesus but not being transformed by the Word is not discipleship, having the clergy do all the care for our congregation is not living out our duty and calling as disciples. We are not suggesting clergy should not show up for the "big stuff" (i.e., major surgeries, death, critical care). However, routine congregational care should be the primary responsibility of the congregation, not a responsibility that we abdicate to clergy. Comforting and caring for fellow congregants is the congregation's duty, responsibility, privilege, and honor. In fact, the clergy can be reappointed at any time, but it is the congregation that sticks around for those long-term relationships. In a small church, the congregation is family or feels like family, which makes it even more important for the care to be done by the congregation.

When transitioning from a pastoral care model to a congregational care model, do so with great mindfulness and communication. Lead with *why* the care model is changing, not *how* the model is changing. Have a couple of people become a point for receiving information and making sure the congregant is adequately being cared for. Consider using resources such as The Caring Congregation Ministry [30] by Karen Lampe and provide training for

---

[30] Karen Lampe and Melissa Collier Gepford, *The Caring Congregation Ministry: Implementation Guide* (Abingdon Press, May 2021).

these point people. Create a well-thought-out communication strategy for the congregation explaining the change. It might even be rolled out with a sermon series using some of the points of Wesley's Sermon 98 or other resources.

Fellowship

Church activities or events grounded in fellowship usually serve the purpose of maintaining relationships with those who are already a part of the congregation. According to thefreedictionary.com, *fellowship* is defined as:

> *a society of people sharing mutual interests, experiences, or activities."* [31]

When researching several resources (i.e., dictionary.com and vocabulary.com) for definitions, many even referenced churches as an example of fellowship. Interestingly enough, *Merriam-Webster*[32] offers the first definition of fellowship as "looking for the fellowship of friendly people" and the second definition as "community of interest, activity, feeling, or experience," but suggests "membership" and "partnership" are now obsolete definitions.

As the country emerges from the pandemic into a new norm of endemic, mental health is a growing concern. According to findings published from a Kaiser Family Foundation[33] poll in October 2022, 47 percent of parents say the pandemic had a negative impact on their child's mental health. Another 51 percent of adults say they or a family member have experienced a severe mental crisis. An overwhelming majority of the public (90 percent) think there is a

---

[31] https://www.thefreedictionary.com/fellowship.

[32] https://www.merriam-webster.com/dictionary/fellowship.

[33] Lunna Lopes, Ashley Kirzinger, Grace Sparks, Mellisha Stokes, and Mollyann Brodie, KFF/CNN *Mental Health in America Survey*, Kaiser Family Foundation, October 05, 2022; https://www.kff.org/report-section/kff-cnn-mental-health-in-america-survey-findings/.

mental health crisis in the U.S. today. Some of the most commonly diagnosed mental disorders are depression and anxiety. People report loneliness and a desire for community.

With the rise of mental health perpetuated by the cocooning of the world's population during the pandemic, there is a tremendous opportunity and calling for churches in our endemic world. If fellowship is no longer described as membership but is now defined as looking for the fellowship of friendly people, aren't churches best equipped for offering such an experience to a lonely world seeking community? And, aren't small churches with the relationship superpower the most equipped to create community with those seeking it? In a hurting world full of so much hate and division, isn't the church the one place in a community that could rise up and be a safe haven for people looking for hope, love, grace, and acceptance?

Nobody does great "comfort food" better than the church! Rather than fellowship dinners being insider events, maybe the easiest way to show love and kindness to your neighbors and friends is to set an extra spot at your table—at home and the next fellowship dinner at church. Extend a personal invitation to join you. Pick them up. Don't ask your guest to bring anything or pay a dime for the meal. Simply love on them. Ask them how they are doing. Make no demands. Set no expectations other than to let you know if they need anything, and you will check in on them to see how they are doing. And then do it.

Instead, we are God's accomplishment,
created in Christ Jesus to do good things.
God planned for these good things to be the way that we live our lives.

Ephesians 2:10 (CEB)

Team Questions

1. What is your primary takeaway from this chapter? How will the leaders begin to simplify the church's approach to ministry?

2. What current ministry can become more relational? How will you approach this shift in the way this ministry is implemented?

3. What one fellowship event will the church consider shifting into an opportunity to build new relationships and love for your neighbors? What is the first step to be taken to begin the shift?

CHAPTER TWELVE

Simplifying Small Church Operations

A church must deal with hundreds of operational details to simply function as a nonprofit entity in the world—finances, incorporation paperwork, website, insurance, child protection policies, membership records, payroll, denominational recordkeeping, building upkeep, church van maintenance, and copyright law. While the complexity involved will be different due to size, a small church of a dozen active members actually has some of the same general expectations as a large church of a thousand in worship. So, as you consider these details, we encourage you to explore ways of simplifying operations to ensure the administration of the church is handled correctly but in a method right-sized for your church.

Whose Church is It?

First, let's be clear. The church is not our private "club." It is not "ours" because the building and property are all dedicated to God to make disciples of Jesus. In our book *IMPACT! Reclaiming the Call of Lay Ministry,* we remind the reader that, regardless of the text on the deed or the trust clause in our *Book of Discipline,* the church is really owned by Jesus Christ:

> *Those of us inside the church must clearly understand to whom the church belongs. The church does not belong to the pastor, the*

lay leaders, the biggest giver, the longest-tenured folks, or even the congregation as a whole. The church belongs to Christ. As Christ followers, we gather to do the work of the church by planting seeds, fertilizing and watering the seeds, and harvesting the crop. We are the laborers—not the owners. When a congregation fully understands this, the potential IMPACT will be far greater! [34]

So, as leaders, our "ownership" is that of caretakers practicing a sacred stewardship of God's resources to fulfill God's mission. The often-misunderstood United Methodist trust clause is much less about ownership than about fidelity to the discipleship mission of Jesus' Church. As trustees, the members of the Leadership Board are fiduciaries responsible for caring for the resources and assets that past and current generations have given God to make disciples for the transformation of the world. In addition to missional accountability, as fiduciaries, it is your responsibility to:

- Make sure that every dollar is used wisely for the highest missional impact.
- The facility is maintained and upgraded as needed for ministry.
- The pastor and any staff are supported and encouraged in the ministry.
- The ministries are run safely.
- The rules, ethical standards, denominational polity, and laws that govern your church are appropriately obeyed.

Finances and Bookkeeping

Unless your church has a knowledgeable member who is excited and willing to manage the church's bookkeeping, produce

---

[34] Kay Kotan and Blake Bradford, *IMPACT! Reclaiming the Call of Lay Ministry,* (Market Square Publishing, May 2018), 15.

reports, and take 365-day-a-year responsibility for the finances, your small church needs to outsource the books to a local accountant. A professional bookkeeper has software to ease the flow of the processes, create reports for the board, cut checks, and ensure that payroll taxes are paid, and the finances are properly managed. Your church is a small client for a bookkeeping business, and the costs will be minimal. Contracting these financial services will unleash more members for ministry and leadership in the church. Contract with a local bookkeeper, assign a few board members as authorized check signers, set expectations for reporting to the board, and let the professional bookkeeper do their thing. Also, you will need to decide how to do the "accounts payable" of tracking and creating statements of offerings for donors—in-house or through the bookkeeper. We suggest having "offering counters" record a Sunday offering count for reconciliation but have the actual tracking of donors and reporting of offerings be the bookkeeper's responsibility.

Having a bookkeeper frees up members for ministry. It relieves the burden of depending on a single member for all this important financial work, which tends to create unhealthy power dynamics in a church where the member has veto power by virtue of their position. Also, the newer methods of giving—including automated fund transfers, online and text-to-give methods, and credit-card giving—require some expertise that will be easier for a bookkeeper to manage. We must come to terms with the fact that the only checks many of us write nowadays are for the church. Most folks we know don't even have a checkbook and don't carry cash. So churches that only receive checks are missing out on opportunities to receive from the generosity of their members and guests.

When interviewing potential bookkeeper candidates, make sure they understand bookkeeping and tax law for nonprofits, particularly churches. You could hire a firm with several staff members or use a single person. One benefit of being a client of a firm is that there will be several eyes on your finances, so there may be more separation of duties. Also, the church is not as dependent on a single person in situations of illness or vacations. That being said, smaller churches have fairly minimal needs.

As an alternative, we have seen some creative partnerships, such as a larger church taking on the bookkeeping services of a small church for free or for a minimal fee to cover the expense. Blake knows of one tiny church that outsources all its finances to the business manager of a larger church, who manages the small church's books as a side gig. In another variation, several churches that share a pastor and staff payroll could contract together with a bookkeeping firm, enabling lower costs for each church.

Getting a bookkeeper to handle the work does not relieve your Leadership Board of the more important governing task of creating a budget. A church budget is not a rigid law; it is a financial flight plan for ministry, which will always be adjusted as needed based on weather conditions. While we have seen churches attempt to simply operate off the balance in their checkbook and their memories about expenses and income in past years, such an approach is inadequate to actually push ministry forward. A budget outlines the priorities of a congregation, making it as much a theological document as a practical one.

We recommend that the church—even small churches—practice fund accounting in which the income lines define the different sources of income (such as plate offerings, rentals, pledged giving, regular unpledged giving) at the top and then the expenses (ministry, staffing, utilities, administration, maintenance, apportionments, insurance, etc.) categorized at the bottom. Ask the bookkeeper to send reports that track these funds from month to month, year to date, and also compare a few years back for context. As a district superintendent, every small church that came to me (Blake) with money troubles had one thing in common: they were not tracking how money was coming into the church or being paid out.

We are often asked if the finance secretary and the treasurer should be ex officio members of the board. As we stated above, the finance secretary and the treasurer are sometimes staff (or contracted labor) and sometimes members volunteering their service and expertise, making them similar to "unpaid staff." So the financial secretary and treasurer should not be treated as members of the Leadership Board but instead treated more like staff or members of ministry teams. Of course, if they are members, they can be elected to the board—multitasking is common in churches, after all. But care should be taken not to see the member who happens to also serve as the financial secretary as the "money person" whose special knowledge of congregational giving becomes the default decider or gatekeeper for all financial matters. They should not have this responsibility or authority.

Concerning the treasurer, there are a few different ways to look at this position's relationship to the board, and a lot depends on congregational culture. The best approach is as follows:

1. Have the treasurer included on a work team with board members to build the budget.

2. Help build the financial section of the Leadership Board packet for the monthly meeting.

3. Be available on a regular basis to report to the board on financial matters or significant expenditures.

4. Be included as part of the process for a certain level of spending in your guiding principles as it relates to cash flow purposes but not approval.

We do not include Leadership Board membership on this list of treasurer jobs because the "money person" often gains an unreasonable amount of power when a voting member of the board. You want the treasurer to report to and be amenable to the board, not be a member.

Words of caution for your consideration: Some faithful disciples unselfishly give their time and talents to care for the bookkeeping needs of their congregation. However, we have also encountered too many treasurers who have used the treasurer's position and the benefit of no term limits to their advantage. Because the treasurer signs the checks, they perceive this as having the power and authority to veto decisions made by the Finance Committee and/or council/ board. While, in actuality, this is not how the *Book of Discipline* is written, the local church sometimes allows this bullying behavior. In other circumstances, the board/council relies on the treasurer to provide an oral report of the current financial picture.

Because every individual has their own values and experiences concerning money, the treasurer can't help but report the finances through their own personal lens. Conversely, when the entire board/ council reviews the financial reports and places several pairs of eyes, perspectives, experiences, and values on the finances, there is a more balanced picture, narrative, and understanding without bias. These are two major reasons why we suggest the treasurer not serve on the board and not attend board meetings for reporting purposes.

There are some great church finance resources in print for churches and pastors. Our favorite is *The Vile Practices of Church Leadership* by Rev. Nate Berneking, treasurer of the Missouri Conference of the United Methodist Church.[35] He details perspectives on stewardship, clergy taxes, and church finances in a clear—and theologically founded—way that is incredibly helpful for the average member in the pew and the seasoned professional. While his book is designed for churches of all sizes, the small church can easily adapt

---

[35] Nate Berneking, *The Vile Practices of Church Leadership: Finance and Administration* (Abingdon Press, May 2017).

from his principles. Nate also explains some complex legal and tax code rules in a very accessible way, a huge help because these rules apply to all churches regardless of size.

The Church Office

Similar to our advice about bookkeeping services, leaders of small churches should consider gig workers, outsourcing, and regional partnerships for other office tasks as well. For instance, we have seen multiple United Methodist churches in a county team up to share a website and an online giving portal. Churches and pastors can team up to buy a group online meeting account. Church landlines can be cut in favor of a cell phone account, making set office hours a thing of the past and lowering the church utility bill.

Creative thinking and new technology can also help connect congregations and clergy together in ways that simply were not possible a few years ago. Microsoft and Google offer their online office suites to small nonprofits for free. Google offers leaders a church email, shared calendars, collaborative online document and spreadsheet creation, and tons of accessible file storage. Providing this kind of technology for small churches equips pastors and leaders with digital tools that enable them to work together without driving to the church. The pastor who commutes from the next town, the part-time church pianist who is the music teacher at the local school, the liturgist assigned for the month, and the youth who sets up sound and technology can collaborate online to build the weekly bulletin document and worship presentation slides, each on their own time from their own home.

The prayer team, pastor, and congregational care team can share a spreadsheet with all those on the prayer and visitation list, along with a private shared calendar on their phones that indicates members' upcoming hospital visits, surgeries, birthdays, and dates of significance which may need a caring follow-up or sympathy card. Files and documents can be stored online for free, allowing members of the Leadership Board and ministry team leaders to access and keep records and pass them quickly to successors. These sorts of tools enable church members to work collaboratively and on their own schedules, making times for actual in-person gatherings and meetings much more productive. They also allow a part-time or bi-vocational pastor to use their time more efficiently. By encouraging collaborative approaches, clergy can perhaps stay out of the "Lone Ranger" mindset that often accompanies the role of clergy in the small church.

Policies and Guidelines

While small churches certainly don't require all the policies that a larger church needs, there are some particular exceptions. First, every church, regardless of size, must have—and diligently follow—written policies for finances and for the protection of children and vulnerable adults. Create right-sized policies for your programs and realistic adult:child supervision ratio numbers that can be followed. You don't want to be in a situation of having a written-but-ignored policy. Talk to the staff at your United Methodist Church annual conference or judicatory body about policy samples for your size church. They may even be able to provide free or low-cost training and background checks for your members who work in youth and children's ministry. It is a sad fact that churches are not immune from those who will abuse our trust. This is not a problem isolated to large churches.

As for financial policies, your United Methodist Church annual conference, judicatory body, or perhaps even a neighboring small church can probably help here as well. You don't have to start from scratch. You will need to include the counting, holding, and depositing of money. For instance, will two unrelated folks count the offering on Sunday before lunch and then send a bank bag home or deliver it to a bank depository? Or will the money be placed in the church's drop safe until Monday? Write down what types of expenses are reimbursed and what documentation is needed. That is not a decision you want to figure out when a member drops by with an unexpected receipt! These financial policies will create and build trust so that everyone will know you are being careful with the money people have donated to make a God-sized impact.

Other policies that might be helpful are a facility use policy and rules for using church resources, such as tables and the church van. In small congregations, church property and buildings are often considered community resources. Every member—right or wrong—has their own key, and folks feel a certain entitlement to just show up to use the building or borrow stuff from the closets. Of course, life happens, and this can create bad feelings among members. It can also prove a bit embarrassing when the "We don't need to reserve the building—I'm a member" child's birthday party conflicts with a funeral in the sanctuary or when the church tables for Sunday's potluck sit in a member's garage after Saturday's yard sale. Create some simple rules, write them down, and make everyone use a reservation calendar. Good fences can make for good neighbors. Similarly, some simple policies can ease some of the friction over resources that naturally occurs in a close-knit church family.

Team Questions

1. Take inventory of the church's current written policies. Do any need to be updated? What policies are missing? Who will create a rough draft of those missing policies to bring to the council/board for editing and approval?

2. Review your current accounting practices and services. Are they currently meeting the needs of the congregation? Are the practices and services provided up to date and taking advantage of modern technology for efficiency? Could outsourcing these services be a better stewardship decision? What steps will the leaders take to improve the financial reporting, practices, and services?

3. What types of technology, services, or other offerings would the church like to improve or add to its operations? How could the church find creative methods to access these? Make a list and choose one or two at a time and slowly improve church operations and their efficiency over time.

SECTION

4

RESOURCES

SCR-1

SAS Discernment Article

Following is a template the church could use in its newsletter to provide an introduction and overview of a simplified, accountable structure during the Discerning Phase.

By unanimous agreement, the Church Council voted (date) to explore moving to a simplified, accountable structure. A subsequent letter was sent to our district superintendent, (name), to request approval for the church to enter into the Discerning Phase for this structure and leadership model. Rev. (DS name) has since approved the church doing so. Pastor (name) and Church Council Chair (name) are in the midst of identifying a Discernment Team to lead the congregation through this discernment process. The Discernment Team will lead the congregation in learning about simplified, accountable structure, answering questions, gaining feedback, sharing FAQs, sharing the steps for implementing the new model, and providing feedback to the Church Council. You'll hear details about the meetings and further information once the Discernment Team has been identified, equipped by our coach, and has created a communication plan to share information.

In the meantime, here is a summary of simplified, accountable structure:

In the United Methodist Church's *Book of Discipline* ¶ 247.2, the church, with approval of the district superintendent, is provided the opportunity to restructure in order to be more missionally focused. This model has now found its way into churches across the country in multiple conferences. It is generally referred to as the simplified structure model. This paragraph was introduced for the primary benefit of small churches that were struggling to have enough people to fill the four administrative committees as required by the traditional structure. Interestingly enough, however, the larger churches were some of the earliest adopters. They quickly identified the efficiency and effectiveness of the model.

To simplify church structure, the four administrative committees (Trustees, Finance, Staff-Parish Relations, and Church Council) cease to exist as we know them currently, and they are replaced by one new Leadership Board of nine people (minimum six in smaller churches when approved by the DS) with three-year terms. This new board is nominated by the Nominations Committee and Lay Leadership Development and voted on by either the church or charge conference. Rather than holding four separate meetings of the four previous administrative committees, there is now one board meeting where the leaders can practice a healthier and more holistic approach with missional focus and direction. Technically, and in fulfillment with the requirements of the *Discipline*, all four committees still exist, but they exist as a single unified Leadership Board, with all of their responsibilities, qualifications, and authority of each administrative committee located in the simplified board.

When simplifying the structure, accountability must be a deeply integrated and highly accepted component of simplification. Without accountability, simplification is not recommended! When transitioning to accountable leadership, the new Leadership Board shifts from managing the church to governing the church.

This significant shift should not be minimized or glossed over. The Leadership Board takes a holistic approach to leadership that is missionally focused on the making of disciples who transform the world (The Great Commission).

Much more information will be shared in the coming weeks. You will have opportunities to have your questions answered as we discern together if this is the right model and the right time for our church. Keep your eyes peeled for informational meeting times to be announced in the coming month.

SCR-2
Simplified, Accountable Structure (SAS) Frequently Asked Questions

1. Which positions can be combined for one person on the Leadership Board to hold?

Most all positions can be combined as long as the minimum number is elected. The lay leader, lay member to annual conference, S/PPR chair, and Trustee chair must be designated, but they could all be the same person.

2. Is there an absolute minimum number for the Leadership Board?

Nine is the standard and recommended minimum. Very small congregations may be able to have a Leadership Board of six, composed of two individuals in each three-year class at the discretion of their district superintendent.

3. Does the pastor have a vote?

No. Because the Leadership Board's work switches roles quickly from Disciplinary committee to committee, we recommend that the pastor not vote in order to preserve clarity and unity on the board. If a matter comes up that depends on one vote of the pastor, that is probably a sign that more conversation and discernment are needed.

4. Can family members serve together on the board?

Per the *Book of Discipline*, family members cannot serve on the board together. If it cannot be avoided, the family members may need to excuse themselves from the room or abstain from voting on issues with a potential conflict of interest. Staff and family of staff cannot serve on the board together.

5. Should staff (paid and unpaid) serve on the board?

No.

6. Who should take notes at the meeting?

Someone not on the board can be assigned or elected to take notes. That person can also be selected from the existing members of the board, a person recruited outside the board to take notes (needs to be excluded from S/PPR conversations), or a person who is an addition to the board with the sole responsibility of taking notes.

7. Are the financial secretary and treasurer required to be on the board?

No, but they can be. The recommendation and best practice are for them NOT to be on the board and interpret their role to be more like (unpaid) staff.

8. Which position on the board serves as the liaison to the district superintendent for Staff/Pastor-Parish Relations Committee purposes?

It is recommended that the board chair serves as the S/PPRC liaison to the DS.

9. Are there still three-year terms and classes?

Yes. One-third of the board will roll off each year.

10. Is the board self-nominating?

No. There is still a requirement for a separate Committee on Nominations and Leadership Development to nominate the board members to the charge conference for election each year.

11. How long can a person serve on the board?

Board members serve a three-year term. Since all members are serving as S/PPR, Trustees, and Finance, it is recommended they roll off after each three-year term. After being off the board for a year, the person can roll back onto the board if elected.

12. Are UMM, UMiF, and UMYF representatives required to be on the board?

If the church has these chartered groups, a member of that group may serve, if requested, on the board as a leader of the local congregation (not to report about their group) and is nominated by the Nominations Committee and elected by the church/charge conference.

13. How many must be present to take an official vote? What requires an official vote?

A quorum is described as whoever is present (Note of exception: in rare matters that require the trustees to function as a legal body, a majority of Leadership Board members who are trustees must be present). A simple majority of Leadership Board members attending approve a motion.

14. How is the Trustee chair elected or appointed as required by the corporate resolution?

At the first meeting at the beginning of each new year, the board will elect a Trustee chair to satisfy the corporate resolution requirement. It is recommended the board chair serve as the Trustee chair. Please note that all board members serving as trustees must be of legal age (eighteen or over in most states). This does not preclude youth under the age of eighteen from serving on the board; they would not be able to vote on any matters of legal consequences.

15. If a church moves to the simplified, accountable structure, how does ministry happen?

Even though the restructuring occurs, ministry teams are still needed and in place. Fewer people on the board mean more people are available to do ministry. Simplifying structure combines the four administrative teams, including the Church Council, Trustees, Finance, and PPPR committees. The only change for ministry teams is that the Nominations Committee is no longer responsible for identifying and nominating leaders and members for ministry teams.

16. Does the church need approval from the district superintendent to move to SAS?

Yes. The first step is to send a letter from the pastor and Council chair to the DS requesting to move to a simplified structure. In the letter, state the missional purpose for moving to this structure. Refer to the Discernment Phase for moving to a simplified, accountable structure. The DS will also need to approve the final structure and authorize the church or charge conference to consider officially transitioning to SAS.

17. Where can I find information on simplified structure in the Book of Discipline?

Paragraph 247.2 in the 2016 edition.

18. How should we pick Leadership Board members? Do we need to seek out people with different skills (i.e., financial, human resources, legal, and marketing)? Should we try to create a team composed of people with personality test results?

By the *Book of Discipline*, all Leadership Board members will need to be professing members of the church since some of the constituent committees require professing membership. The right team is composed of devoted disciples of Jesus who can think strategically about the church's mission; hold clergy, staff, and fellow members accountable to the mission; and partner with other Leadership Board members to guide the congregation into making a God-sized impact.

The Leadership Board should be as diverse as possible so that the leadership table will have the different voices that God needs for the congregation to discern its future direction. Other skills can be added through work groups. While teams can be designed using a variety of tools, don't let these tools get in the way of the fact that Jesus' mission needs Jesus' disciples, and accountability must come before any other considerations.

19. What size church is too small or too large for SAS?

While ¶ 247.2 was written for small churches that had difficulty finding enough people to fill all the "slots" in a traditional committee structure, some of our largest churches first discovered the power, efficiency, and effectiveness of SAS. Churches with an average worship attendance under fifty may already be doing a de facto simplified structure, and they may or may not be using accountability. Large churches that worship in the thousands have discovered the need for SAS as they seek to counteract ministry silos and missional drift. Mid-size congregations from one hundred to five hundred in worship will quickly discover the power of SAS in unleashing more laity for ministry and focusing the church on Christ's mission.

20. What are the Discipline requirements for Leadership Board composition?

The Leadership Board should consist of professing members, with a *Discipline*-recommended minimum of one-third being laywomen and one-third being laymen.

21. Who can attend the meetings?

Congregation members are always invited to attend the meetings but do not have a voice or vote. When the need arises for the Leadership Board to move into executive session to address S/PPRC matters or to consider legal negotiations (such as buying or selling property), congregational members not elected to the board will need to be excused.

21. Should we assign Leadership Board members to specialist roles for finance or personnel?

No! This defeats the purpose of the simplified structure and interrupts Leadership Board accountability. While the board may assign a work group to work on a special project and report back, only the entire Leadership Board has the responsibility and authority to act and make decisions.

SCR-3
Organizational Chart for the Small Church

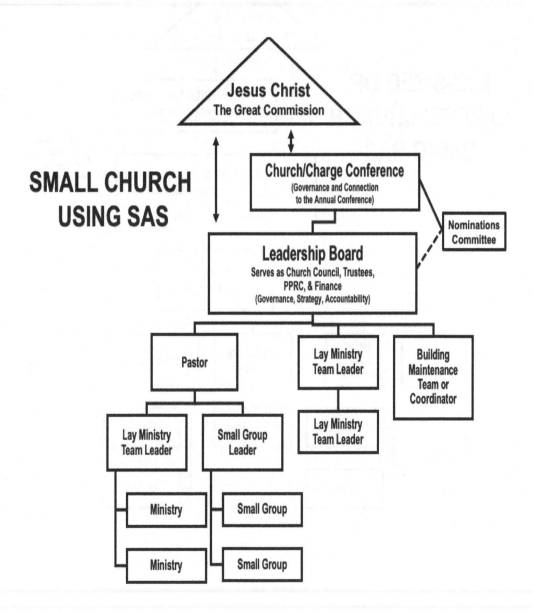

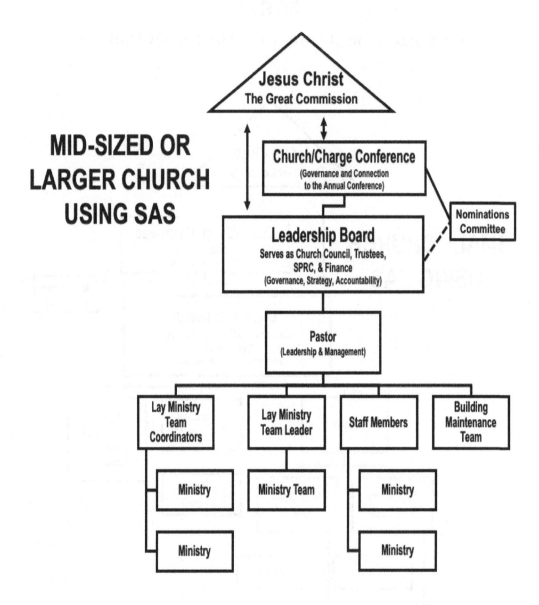

MID-SIZED OR LARGER CHURCH USING SAS

Jesus Christ
The Great Commission

Church/Charge Conference
(Governance and Connection to the Annual Conference)

Nominations Committee

Leadership Board
Serves as Church Council, Trustees, SPRC, & Finance
(Governance, Strategy, Accountability)

Pastor
(Leadership & Management)

Lay Ministry Team Coordinators

Lay Ministry Team Leader

Staff Members

Building Maintenance Team

Ministry

Ministry Team

Ministry

Ministry

Ministry

SCR-4

Nominations Tool

20__ Nominations
Simplified, Accountable Structure

Church

The use of this simplified structure is allowed by ¶ 247.2 of the *2016 Book of Discipline* with district superintendent approval. Indicate (ROLE) which member is serving as Chair (C), Lay Leader (LL), and Lay Member to Annual Conference (LMAC). It is HIGHLY recommended that the board chair serves as the DS liaison for HR purposes.

The following persons will serve as the governing board, fulfilling the Disciplinary roles and responsibilities of Church Council, Trustees, Finance, and Staff/Pastor-Parish Relations Committee

Term to Serve	Person's Name	Phone Number	Person's Email	Role Chair, LL, LMAC, UWF, UMM, UMY
Class of 2024				
Class of 2025				
Class of 2026				

All Leadership Board members will need to be professing members.
Youth under eighteen cannot serve as trustees.
The final board must be at least one-third laymen and one-third laywomen, so it is recommended that each class contain
at least one man and one woman.
Staff and household members of staff cannot serve on the board.

Committee on Nominations and Leadership Development

¶ 258.1 – The committee is composed of not more than nine persons in addition to the pastor and lay leader. It shall include at least one young adult and may include one or more youth.

Pastor (Chairperson) and Lay Leader		
Class of 2024	**Class of 2025**	**Class of 2026**

Charge Conference Elected Officers for District and Conference Records

Note: In the Simplified Accountable Structure for small churches, multiple roles listed below will usually be filled by the same individual. These positions are listed separately for database management purposes for the district and conference.

Officers	Person's Name	Phone Number	Person's Email
Lay Member of Annual Conference			
Trustee Chair			
Lay Leader			
PPRC Contact for District Superintendent			
Treasurer (Tracks Spending)			
Financial Secretary (Tracks Income)			

By *Discipline,* the "Trustee Chair" is elected by the "Trustees" (Leadership Board who has BOD authority and responsibility as trustees and legal board of directors) at their first meeting of every year, so please contact your district office to update or confirm your church's leadership record following the election.

By *Discipline,* the Treasurer and the Finance Secretary cannot be the same person.

SCR-5

Resolution for the Small Church

The Committee on Nominations and Leadership Development, in coordination with the Administrative Board, moves the charge/church conference adoption of a resolution to modify our organizational plan of governance, utilizing the simplified, accountable structure:

Resolution to Change Congregational Organizational Plan to Simplified, Accountable Governance Structure

WHEREAS, ¶ 247.2 of the *2016 Book of Discipline for the United Methodist Church* allows alternative models of governance℠; and

WHEREAS, the simplified, accountable leadership structure is utilized as an alternative model throughout the denomination and fulfills the provisions℠℠ of ¶ 243 of the *2016 Book of Discipline for the United Methodist Church;* and

WHEREAS, the Church Council of _____ United Methodist Church prayerfully voted on (date) to explore the simplified, accountable structure for local church governance; and

WHEREAS, the congregation provided feedback concerning a potential change in governance structure on multiple occasions; and

WHEREAS, the congregation was motivated to convert for reasons of efficiency, alignment with our mission and vision, accountability, and missional focus; and

WHEREAS, the Church Council, Committee on Nominations and Leadership Development, [the task force on governance], and the pastor, after months of discernment, have crafted an alternative organizational and governance structure for _____ United Methodist Methodist Church and offered this proposal to the district superintendent for approval; and

WHEREAS, the district superintendent approved the alternative organizational plan on (date); and

NOW, THEREFORE, BE IT RESOLVED THAT:

Resource from *Mission Possible for the Small Church* by Kay Kotan and Blake Bradford, Market Square Publishing, 2023.
Permission to copy for use with *Mission Possible for the Small Church*.

1. On January 1, 20__, the Disciplinary authority and various responsibilities of the Church Council, Staff-Parish Relations Committee (SPRC), Finance Committee, Endowment Committee, and Board of Trustees, will be combined into a single body called the Leadership Board.[36] Existing elected leadership of all classes of all constituent committees that make up the new Leadership Board will conclude their terms of service on December 31, 20__, as the church transitions to the new organizational plan.

2. The Committee on Nominations and Leadership Development of _____ United Methodist Church is directed to submit a list of officers and members of a simplified, accountable structure known as the Leadership Board and a Committee on Nominations and Leadership Development, divided into appropriate three-year classes, as outlined in the *Discipline*, for election by the charge conference. All members of the Leadership Board and the charge conference will be professing members. The chair of the Board of Trustees will be elected from among the voting trustee members of the Leadership Board in the first board meeting of each year, in accordance with the *Discipline*, and s/he may be the Leadership Board chair.

3. On January 1, 20__, the charge conference of _____ United Methodist Church will be composed of the members of the Leadership Board, appointed clergy (ex-officio), together with retired ordained ministers and retired diaconal ministers who elect to hold their membership in our charge conference, lay members of annual conference, the lay leader, treasurer, and finance secretary (if non-staff), and the elected membership of the Committee on Nominations and Leadership Development.

4. The lay member of annual conference and lay leader are ex officio members of the Leadership Board, if not already elected into a membership class of the Leadership Board.

5. All Disciplinary requirements and qualifications for each of the constituent committees (Church Council, SPRC, Finance Committee, and Board of Trustees) will continue with the combined Leadership Board, including trustee age-of-majority qualifications and SPRC household membership limitations.

---

[36] ¶ 247.2 The charge conference, the district superintendent, and the pastor, when a pastor has been appointed (see ¶ 205.4), shall organize and administer the pastoral charge and churches according to the policies and plans herein set forth. When the membership size, program scope, mission resources, or other circumstances so require, the charge conference may, in consultation with and upon the approval of the district superintendent, modify the organizational plans, provided that the provisions of ¶ 243 are observed. Such other circumstances may include, but not be limited to, alternative models for the conception of a local church, such as coffeehouse ministries, mall ministries, outdoor ministries, retirement home ministries, restaurant ministries, and other emergent ways in which people can gather in God's name to be the church.

Resource from *Mission Possible for the Small Church* by Kay Kotan and Blake Bradford, Market Square Publishing, 2023. Permission to copy for use with *Mission Possible for the Small Church*.

6. All references to the Church Council, Board of Trustees, SPRC, and Finance Committee, in all existing church policies, as of December 31, 20__, shall be understood to refer to the Leadership Board beginning January 1, 20__.

7. The Board of Trustees is directed immediately to make appropriate amendments to the congregation's bylaws to reflect the new plan for organization and submit an update to the Secretary of State's office in a manner defined by state law for nonprofit corporations.

8. In service to our common mission to make disciples of Jesus Christ for the transformation of the world, all existing ministry teams will be accountable to the pastor and Leadership Board in administrative matters and in fulfillment of ¶ 243.[37] The Weekday Child-Care Ministry Advisory Board (¶ 256.2c) will be amenable to the Leadership Board in all matters and is responsible for regular reporting to the board. Alternative: If the Weekday Child-Care Ministry is not a separate 501(c)(3), this Advisory Board will be a ministry team and accountable directly to the pastor.

9. The Leadership Board will abide by existing financial, child protection, building use, personnel policies, and the inaugural guiding principles. The board will create a Leadership Board Covenant. The Leadership Board is empowered to amend these policies, principles, and covenants. The Leadership Board shall share updated guiding principles with the charge conference annually.

APPROVED, (date).

_____   _____
Secretary, Charge Conference   Presiding Elder

---

[37] ¶ 243. Primary Tasks—The local church shall be organized so that it can pursue its primary task and mission in the context of its own community—reaching out and receiving with joy all who will respond; encouraging people in their relationship with God and inviting them to commitment to God's love in Jesus Christ; providing opportunities for them to seek strengthening and growth in spiritual formation; and supporting them to live lovingly and justly in the power of the Holy Spirit as faithful disciples.In carrying out its primary task, it shall be organized so that adequate provision is made for these basic responsibilities: (1) planning and implementing a program of nurture, outreach, and witness for persons and families within and without the congregation; (2) providing for effective pastoral and lay leadership; (3) providing for financial support, physical facilities, and the legal obligations of the church; (4) utilizing the appropriate relationships and resources of the district and annual conference; (5) providing for the proper creation, maintenance, and disposition of documentary record material of the local church; and (6) seeking inclusiveness in all aspects of its life.

SCR-6
Sample Leadership Board Covenant

The Rules of the Road
A Leadership Board Covenant for the Small Church

Decisions are Made by the Board Members Who Attend:

- The Leadership Board and Committee on Nominations and Leadership Development are elected by the charge conference in accordance with the *Book of Discipline of the United Methodist Church*.

- Except for official Trustee legal business (which has a majority attendance requirement for a quorum), the *Discipline* defines a quorum as those members of a committee who are present.

- Leadership Board members are expected to attend all board meetings unless ill or out of town. If needed, members can be tied into meetings via speaker phones or video chat. If members miss more than three meetings per year, the board chair will converse with the board member to see if their seat needs to be vacated and filled by someone who can be more active.

- Teleconference or online meeting participation is okay if allowed by the group, but the United Methodist Church does not authorize voting "proxies."

- The board will move into a confidential "executive session" whenever Pastor-Parish Relations Committee work is being done. Only official PPRC members can be present for that component of the meeting, and all the appropriate PPRC restrictions of the *Book of Discipline* apply.

- Leadership Board members will review the meeting packet prior to meetings coming fully prepared and ready to participate.

- During a duly called and advertised meeting, we don't delay board business because someone is missing unless there are extenuating circumstances, such as foul weather.

Leadership Board Members are Disciples of Jesus and Fiduciary Officers:

- Board members carry, support, and promote the mission and vision of the church at all times.

- Leadership Board members are role models for the congregation. Therefore, members will model mature discipleship by being present in worship at least three times per month, giving proportionally, having an active prayer life, serving in mission three times per year, being active on a ministry team, being in a consistent faith development group, and openly sharing their faith with others in the secular world.

- Leadership Board members will encourage and support their pastor and fellow board members.

- Leadership Board members will hold themselves, the pastor, and other board members accountable for their leadership roles and responsibilities. This includes allowing others to hold the board members collectively and individually accountable.

- Leadership Board members shall recuse themselves from any situation that could be construed as a conflict of interest.

- Leadership Board members have no special or unique personal authority or ability to demand time or actions from the pastor or staff outside that assigned by the Leadership Board.

- Leadership Board members will act in good faith, serving out of loyalty to the mission of the church, obedience to the *Book of Discipline of the United Methodist Church* and policies set forth by the charge conference and annual conference, and faithfulness to their duties as board members.

- Leadership Board members hold one another in daily prayer.

We Will Speak the Truth in Love (Ephesians 4:15)

- Communication will be respectful, open, and honest. As a Leadership Board, we will approach matters of disagreement with transparency and maintain our missional focus on making disciples of Jesus Christ. Board members will not participate in parking lot conversations regarding our role as a board member.

- Leadership Board members understand that conflict and disagreements are natural in any community, including the church. When approached by a person or group concerning a matter of disagreement or conflict, we will follow the path laid out by Jesus in Matthew 18 by encouraging the concerned party to go directly to the individual or by volunteering to go with the concerned party as an supportive presence. In accordance with the *Book of Discipline of the United Methodist Church,* the pastor will be present in all meetings unless the pastor is voluntarily absent. At no time will we support or participate in secret meetings that undermine the integrity or authority of the pastor or the Leadership Board.

- Leadership Board members are representatives of the Leadership Board at all times during their leadership terms. Leadership Board members have a fiduciary duty to the Leadership Board and the church to uphold the highest standards of integrity of relationships and to support the mission of the congregation, including publicly supporting other congregational leaders, staff, ministry leaders, and clergy of the congregation.

- Leadership Board members will hold each other accountable as disciples of Jesus and church leaders through our prayers, presence, gifts, service, and witness.

- The Leadership Board (in its role of PPRC) will hold the pastor accountable in collaboration with the bishop and district superintendent.

We Will Balance Transparency and Confidentiality

- The United Methodist Church supports open meetings (*BOD* ¶ 722) at all levels of the church. Exceptions are Pastor-Parish Relations Committee work and some legal work of the Trustees, such as property negotiations.

- In its role and responsibility as the Pastor-Parish Relations Committee, the Leadership Board is held to a high standard of confidentiality in personnel and clergy appointment matters.

- Board members understand that as leaders, derogatory comments or conversations about personnel (especially the pastor) are inappropriate and to be avoided. Concerns are to be processed with the collective Leadership Board and the district superintendent only.

- The Leadership Board will move into executive session for some agenda items, particularly the work as the Pastor-Parish Relations Committee. In those cases, a separate set of minutes for the session shall be kept, and those not on the board should be excused from the meeting.

- No secret meetings are allowed, and when the Leadership Board is doing the business of the Pastor-Parish Relations Committee, the pastor shall be present (see *BOD* ¶ 258.2 for particulars).

We are a Leadership Board with a Unified Voice

- Leadership Board members are encouraged to invest in board conversations and decisions with vigor and passion. However, once the board has come to a decision, each Leadership Board member will openly and publicly support the decision of the Leadership Board whether the individual member personally agrees with the decision. A unified voice and message from the Leadership Board are essential.

- Board members will not call out or undermine the collective decisions of the board.

SCR-7
Sample Guiding Principles

The following guiding principles are offered to you as guidelines or thought-starters. These are not intended to be a complete set of building principles. In fact, you will find that a few guiding principles contradict one another. This is intentional and is offered to remind churches of the importance of clarity around specific guiding principles. Guiding principles are intended to be a permission-giving tool. They eleiminate a drawn-out approval process and any bottleneck that slows down ministry. Guiding principles provide healthy boundaries and macro, rather than micro, decision-making. Please do not cut and paste these (or other churches') guiding principles. Every church has its own unique setting, so special care and attention in this work will pay dividends for years to come.

- All references to the Church Council, Board of Trustees, Staff/Pastor-Parish Relations Committee, Endowment Committee, and Finance Committee, in all congregational policies as of _____, and in all references in the *Book of Discipline of the United Methodist Church,* shall be understood to refer to the Leadership Board beginning _____.

- Once the budget is approved, those responsible (i.e., staff and team leaders) for the various ministry areas have the authority to spend their budget to align with the objectives for their ministry area approved by the pastor. No further approval is needed to access the budget in their area of responsibility.*

- The pastor is responsible for reviewing line items within ministry areas with the appropriate staff or team leaders for accountability from the staff and to the board.

- Any member of the Building Maintenance Team has the authority to purchase supplies for building maintenance and improvement up to $ _____ without approval. The Building Maintenance Team leader can authorize purchases for building maintenance and improvement up to $ _____. Purchases up to $ _____ can be approved by the pastor (executive pastor or business manager). Any purchases over $ _____ need Leadership Board approval unless the expenditure is already approved in a capital expenditure line item in the approved budget.*

- Any expenditure over $ _____ will require three bids. Preference will be given to hiring local companies offering competitive bids within ___% of other bids. If the expenditure is already approved in the budget and meets the previous criteria, no further approval is needed. The ministry team leader or staff member responsible for the purchase will provide documentation of the bids to the Leadership Board for purposes of a paper trail only.

*The treasurer must be consulted concerning any single purchase or expenditure over $_____ for purposes of cash flow. The treasurer does not approve or deny purchases but confirms large purchases will not create cash flow issues.

- The pastor has the authority to hire and release employees using the church's employee policies and procedures in the _____ *UMC Employee Handbook*. When terminating an employee, the pastor will invite a board member to sit in on the exit conversation for purposes of liability protection. The pastor is responsible for supervising, disciplining, and evaluating staff performance as outlined in the _____ *UMC Employee Handbook*.

- The authority to hire and terminate employees of the church shall be vested in the Leadership Board. The pastor shall have the authority to interview and recommend candidates to fill open staff positions. The board shall have the sole authority to determine the number of staff positions, approve job descriptions for each staff member, and set the salary paid to each staff member. The Leadership Board delegates the authority to supervise, discipline, and manage paid staff to the pastor.

- The pastor will review all paid staff annually using the approval evaluation process in the employee manual dated _____.

- The board recognizes and approves the Building Usage Policies dated _____.

- The board recognizes and approves the Building Security and Key Policies dated _____.

- The board recognizes and approves the Financial Controls Policies dated _____.

- The board recognizes and approves the _____ United Methodist Church Personnel Policies date _____.

- All meetings of the Leadership Board shall be open to the public, except for any meeting or portion of a meeting in which a personnel matter or a matter of legal negotiations is considered. In those cases, the board will transition into executive session. Minutes of executive session agenda items concerning personnel matters will be kept separately as part of the "S/PPRC" files.

- Leadership Board members are nominated by a separate and independent Committee on Nominations and Leadership Development, chaired by the pastor, and elected by the charge conference as described in the *Book of Discipline*. The Nominations Committee will be responsible for developing new leaders and equipping them for future Leadership Board positions.

- Due to the Leadership Board's serving as the congregation's Staff-Parish Relations Committee, no immediate family member of the pastor or other paid staff person may serve as a board member. Due to serving as the congregation's Board of Trustees, only Leadership Board members over the age of eighteen will have voting privileges in matters of property, incorporation, legal matters, contracts, insurance, investments, or other matters described in the *BOD* ¶s 2525-2551.

- The lead pastor is the Leadership Board's only link to church ministry and programming. The lead pastor has complete authority and accountability for all staffing, including hiring, evaluating, firing, and consideration of raises. The Council will never give instructions to persons who report directly or indirectly to the lead pastor. The Council will view the lead pastor's performance as identical to church performance so that organizational goals will be viewed as the lead pastor's performance.

- Compensation for the lead pastor and all appointed clergy will be determined by a charge/church conference. Recommendations for the lead pastor's compensation will be made by the Leadership Board (as part of their SPRC duties) to the entire Church Council for consideration before the charge/church conference. Recommendations for other appointed clergy compensation will be made by the lead pastor in consultation with the Leadership Board to the entire Church Council for consideration before the charge/church conference. Decisions about increases in the lead pastor's compensation will be based primarily on the following three criteria:

  1. Council's review of the lead pastor's effectiveness in reaching established goals.

  2. Needs of the church for a lead pastor with the skill sets necessary for reaching established goals. This will be determined in relation to the compensation packages of churches of similar or larger size in the annual conference.

  3. Possible cost of living increases. However, it is understood that the primary criteria for compensation will always be (a) the Leadership Board's review of the lead pastor's performance.

- The lead pastor shall not cause or allow any activity, decision, or organizational circumstance that is unlawful or in violation of commonly accepted business practices and professional ethics. Furthermore, the lead pastor shall not cause or allow any activity, decision, or organizational circumstance that is a violation of the current *Book of Discipline*, the standing rules of the annual conference, or the express direction of the resident bishop and/or district superintendent of the annual conference.

SCR-8

Sample Agenda for the Small Church

First United Methodist Church
Leadership Board Meeting

Date _____

Our Mission: To make new disciples of Jesus Christ for the transformation of the world.

Our Vision: Each of us at _____ UMC is on a journey to grow closer to God, to be more like Jesus, and to be filled with the Holy Spirit. No matter where you are in your walk with Christ, you are invited to journey and grow with us through the power of the Holy Spirit so that we can fulfill God's commission.

Core Values:

- Encouragement - Giving hope to people who need some hope
- Excellence - Maintaining the highest of ministry standards that bring glory to God
- Fellowship - Relating to and enjoying one another
- Aspiring Core Value is Evangelism - Telling others the good news about Christ

Opening Prayer

Spiritual Formation

Leadership Development

Consent Calendar Items

Fiduciary Work

Missional Accountability Work

Strategic and Planning Work

Pressing Issues/Problem-Solving

Executive Session (PPRC)

Communication

Closing Prayer

SCR-9
Simple Planning for the Small Church

- **We, Not They** – "All Hands on Deck" is the rule, not the exception, so plan with all active attendees of all ages being involved in implementing the ministry.

- **Get Face-to-Face** – Focus on building relationships, not complex systems.

- **Evangelism is not an Extra** – Embed evangelism (reaching new people for Jesus) into every ministry, every event, and every opportunity.

- **Dream Up a Team Up** – Partner with local institutions and nonprofits, especially for organizing the infrastructure for community ministry, leaning on their expertise and organization.

- **Deep, Not Wide** – Who is God calling you to build relationships with? Choose one niche and go deep relationally and with ministries for this one group. You'll reach more people using fewer resources without burning your volunteers out.

- **When in Doubt, Experiment** – Allow yourselves to try ministry experiments. In a season when many of our inherited ways of doing ministry are no longer effective, try something new every season or at least twice a year.

- **Simple with a Signature** – Instead of having multiple low-impact ministries, take a simple approach by discerning and focusing on one or two signature ministries.

- **Keep Accountable** – Be good stewards of God's people and resources by pruning ministries regularly and using the "Accountable Leadership Cycle" to keep the church on track and always learning.

Other Books by Kay Kotan and Blake Bradford

MISSION POSSIBLE 3+

EXPANDED THIRD EDITION!
New Resources, Activities, and Checklists

MISSION: POSSIBLE

A Simple Structure for Missional Effectiveness

Kay Kotan & Blake Bradford

marketsquarebooks.com